# 『メルケル首相の理想と課題』正誤表

下記のように訂正し、お詫び申し上げます。

○89ページ　上から4行目

（誤）　関係していますか。

↓

（正）　関係していますか。

*Spiritual Interview
with the Guardian
Spirit of Angela*
*Merkel*

スピリチュアル・インタビュー

# メルケル首相の
# 理想と課題

RYUHO OKAWA
大川隆法

本霊言は、2018年9月28日、幸福の科学 特別説法堂にて、
公開収録された(写真)。

スピリチュアル・インタビュー

メルケル首相の理想と課題

# Spiritual Interview with the Guardian Spirit of Angela Merkel

*Preface*

On October 7, 2018, I gave an English lecture titled "Love for the Future" in Berlin, Germany. This book is the spiritual messages from the Guardian Spirit of Chancellor Merkel recorded in Tokyo about 10 days before the lecture with the aim of finding her real mind.

The basic way of thinking and mentality of Chancellor Merkel has been revealed through this book. Also, it clearly shows why her way of thinking conflicts with the American President Donald Trump.

I, myself, thought that Ms. Merkel was essentially a physicist from East Germany, but everything became clear to me after I found out that she was a great and honorable philosopher of Germany in her past life. The longest-reigning female chancellor-to-be and the de facto head of the EU is also a philosopher in a struggle between theory and practice.

まえがき

　私は 2018 年 10 月 7 日、ドイツはベルリンで "Love for the Future" と題する英語講演を行った。本書は、その 10 日ほど前に、メルケル首相の本心を探る目的で、東京で行われた守護霊霊言である。

　本書によって、メルケル首相の基本的考え方や精神性は明確になった。また、なぜアメリカのドナルド・トランプ大統領と考え方が対立するのかも明白になった。

　私自身、東独出身の物理学者がメルケル氏の本質だと思っていたが、ドイツが誇る大哲学者が過去世だと判り、すべてに納得がいった。最長政権になるであろう女性首相にして、EU の事実上のトップが、理論と実際の間で苦闘する哲学者でもあったのだ。

In yesterday's news, Ms. Merkel announced her resignation as a party leader after losing twice in a row in regional elections. Her term as a chancellor lasts until fall 2021, so I just wish her the best of luck.

Oct. 30, 2018

Master & CEO of Happy Science Group

Ryuho Okawa

昨日のニュースでは、メルケル氏は地方選の２連敗を契機に、党首を辞めるとのことだ。首相としての任期は2021年秋まであるが、幸多からんことを祈るばかりである。


2018 年 10 月 30 日

幸福の科学グループ創始者兼総裁

大川隆法

# Contents

Preface ......................................................................................................... 2

1   Inspiration of an Astonishing Spiritual Interview ........................ 16

2   "My Aim is to Make
One Organization for World Peace" ....................................... 20

3   Views on Trump, Xi Jinping, and Putin ............................... 48

4   Can We Change the Regime of
China, a Country of No God? ................................................ 58

5   Any Good Policies for the German Economy? ...................... 78

6   Where Did Nazism Come From? ........................................... 88

7   "My Dream in the Next Century is
'a Global-Level Government'" ............................................... 94

8   What Merkel's Guardian Spirit
Thinks of National Security ................................................ 106

9   Views on Confucianism and Prime Minister Abe ............... 116

# 目　次

まえがき ………………………………………………………………　3

1　驚愕の内容を秘めた霊言の予感 ……………………17

2　目指すのは「世界平和のための単一組織」……………… 21

3　トランプ、習近平、プーチンをどう見ているか ……… 49

4　「神なき中国」の体制を変えられるか ……………………… 59

5　ドイツ経済の良策はあるか ………………………………… 79

6　ナチズムの思想的淵源を分析する ……………………… 89

7　来世紀の夢は「地球レベルの政府」……………………… 95

8　メルケル守護霊の安全保障の考え方は ………………… 107

9　儒教と安倍首相に対する見方 …………………………… 117

10 Merkel's Past Life—
a Great Philosopher Who Sought for Perpetual Peace ········ 126

11 After the Spiritual Interview ·················································· 148

* This spiritual interview was conducted in English. The Japanese text is a translation.

10 前世は「永遠平和」を希求した大哲学者 …………………… 127

11 霊言を終えて ………………………………………………………………… 149

※本書は、英語で収録された霊言に和訳を付けたものです。

This book is the transcript of spiritual interview with the guardian spirit of Chancellor Angela Merkel of Germany.

These spiritual messages were channeled through Ryuho Okawa. However, please note that because of his high level of enlightenment, his way of receiving spiritual messages is fundamentally different from other psychic mediums who undergo trances and are completely taken over by the spirits they are channeling.

Each human soul is generally made up of six soul siblings, one of whom acts as the guardian spirit of the person living on earth. People living on earth are connected to their guardian spirits at the innermost subconscious level. They are a part of people's very souls and therefore exact reflections of their thoughts and philosophies.

It should be noted that these spiritual messages are opinions of the individual spirits and may contradict the ideas or teachings of the Happy Science Group.

本書は、ドイツのアンゲラ・メルケル首相の守護霊霊言を収録したものである。

　「霊言現象」とは、あの世の霊存在の言葉を語り下ろす現象のことをいう。これは高度な悟りを開いた者に特有のものであり、「霊媒現象」（トランス状態になって意識を失い、霊が一方的にしゃべる現象）とは異なる。

　また、人間の魂は原則として６人のグループからなり、あの世に残っている「魂の兄弟」の１人が守護霊を務めている。つまり、守護霊は、実は自分自身の魂の一部である。

　したがって、「守護霊の霊言」とは、いわば、本人の潜在意識にアクセスしたものであり、その内容は、その人が潜在意識で考えていること（本心）と考えてよい。

　ただ、「霊言」は、あくまでも霊人の意見であり、幸福の科学グループとしての見解と矛盾する内容を含む場合がある点、付記しておきたい。

# Spiritual Interview with the Guardian Spirit of Angela Merkel

September 28, 2018 at Special Lecture Hall, Happy Science, Tokyo

# スピリチュアル・インタビュー
## メルケル首相の理想と課題

2018 年 9 月 28 日　東京都・幸福の科学特別説法堂にて

## Angela Merkel (1954 – Present)

A German politician born in West Germany. Moved to East Germany, a socialist country, after her father, a pastor, was offered a position at a church in East Berlin, where she then spent her early years. Merkel majored in physics at Karl Marx University, Leipzig (currently the University of Leipzig). After graduation, she went on to work at the Academy of Sciences, where she pursued her research in theoretical physics. Merkel took interest in politics after the fall of the Berlin Wall in 1989 and was successfully elected in the German federal election in 1990. She was appointed the leader of the Christian Democratic Union (CDU) in 2000. In 2005, Merkel became the chancellor of Germany; she is now serving her fourth term. She is the first female chancellor in German history. Merkel has been ranked first for seven consecutive years in "The World's 100 Most Powerful Women" list by *Forbes*.

### Interviewers from Happy Science

Masayuki Isono

Executive Director
Chief of Overseas Missionary Work Promotion Office
Deputy Chief Secretary, First Secretarial Division
Religious Affairs Headquarters

Jiro Ayaori

Managing Director
Director General of Magazine Editing Division
Chief Editor of *The Liberty*
Lecturer, Happy Science University

Hanako Cho

Deputy General Manager of Magazine Editing Division
Lecturer, Happy Science University

★ Interviewers are listed in the order that they appear in the transcript.
 Their professional titles represent their positions at the time of the interview.

## アンゲラ・メルケル （1954 ～）

ドイツの政治家。西ドイツに生まれる。牧師だった父が東ベルリンの教会に赴任することになり、東ドイツに移住。社会主義の同国で育つ。カールマルクス・ライプツィヒ大学（現ライプツィヒ大学）で物理学を専攻。卒業後、科学アカデミーに就職し、理論物理学を研究する。1989 年、ベルリンの壁が崩壊すると政治に関心を持ち、翌年、連邦議会選挙に出馬して初当選した。2000 年、ドイツキリスト教民主同盟（CDU）の党首に就任。05 年、首相となり、現在 4 期目。ドイツ史上初の女性首相であり、アメリカの雑誌「フォーブス」の「世界で最も影響力のある女性」ランキングで 7 年連続 1 位に選ばれている。

#### 質問者（幸福の科学）

磯野将之 （理事 兼 宗務本部海外伝道推進室長 兼 第一秘書局担当局長）

綾織次郎 （常務理事 兼 総合誌編集局長 兼 「ザ・リバティ」 編集長 兼 HSU 講師）

長華子 （総合誌編集局担当部長代理 兼 HSU 講師）

※質問順。役職は収録当時のもの。

# 1 Inspiration of an Astonishing Spiritual Interview

**Ryuho Okawa** We'd like to challenge, "Spiritual Interview with the Guardian Spirit of Chancellor Merkel of Germany." She's the most powerful lady in the world, as you know. My inspiration says today will be an astonishing day, but you will know the conclusion at the end of this session. If you have enough power to converse with her, you are very respectable people, I think so.

To tell the truth, her guardian spirit can speak Japanese, but it's a secret. We must have a lesson speaking in English, so I'll never speak in Japanese [*laughs*]. I'll do my best, but she can understand Japanese. OK? Then, I'll call her.

[*Takes a deep breath.*]

# 1　驚愕の内容を秘めた霊言の予感

大川隆法　「ドイツのメルケル首相の守護霊インタビュー」に挑戦してみたいと思います。ご存じの通り、世界で最もパワフルな女性です。私の直感では、今日は驚愕の一日になりそうですが、結論はこのセッションの最後にわかるでしょう。あなたがたに彼女と会話をするだけの力が十分あるなら、大したものだと思います。

　実を言うと、彼女の守護霊は日本語を話せるのですが、それは秘密でございまして。英語で話す練習をしないといけませんので、私は絶対、日本語は話しません（笑）。できるだけやってみますが、日本語がわかる方です。よろしいですか。では、お呼びします。

（深く深呼吸）

1 Inspiration of an Astonishing Spiritual Interview

Could I summon the guardian spirit of Angela Merkel? Could I summon the guardian spirit of Angela Merkel in Deutschland? The chancellor's guardian spirit, would you come down here? The guardian spirit of Angela Merkel.

[*About 12 seconds of silence.*]

アンゲラ・メルケルの守護霊をお呼びいたします。ドイツのアンゲラ・メルケルの守護霊をお呼びいたします。首相の守護霊よ、ご降臨ください。アンゲラ・メルケルさんの守護霊よ。


（約12秒間の沈黙）

## 2 "My Aim is to Make One Organization for World Peace"

**Angela Merkel's Guardian Spirit** Uh. *Guten Morgen* ("Good morning" in German).

**Masayuki Isono** Guten Morgen. Are you the guardian spirit of Chancellor Merkel?

**Merkel's G.S.** Yeah.

**Isono** Thank you very much for coming to Happy Science today. We are so happy to have you here. I'm so excited to have a talk with you. Thank you very much.

**Merkel's G.S.** Be cool.

**Isono** Be cool? Be good?

## 2　目指すのは「世界平和のための単一組織」

アンゲラ・メルケル守護霊　うん。グーテン・モルゲン（ドイツ語で「おはようございます」）。

磯野将之　グーテン・モルゲン。メルケル首相の守護霊様でいらっしゃいますでしょうか。

メルケル守護霊　はい。

磯野　本日は、ようこそ幸福の科学にお越しくださいました。お迎えすることができ、大変光栄です。お話しさせていただけるので非常に興奮しております。ありがとうございます。

メルケル守護霊　冷静にね。

磯野　クール？　グッド？

**Merkel's G.S.** Cool. Cool.

**Isono** OK. Be cool.

**Merkel's G.S.** Behave yourself.

**Isono** OK. Behave myself. OK. You became the first female chancellor in 2005. Since then, you have led Germany, the most powerful country of the EU, for these 13 years.

**Merkel's G.S.** Thank you, thank you, thank you very much.

**Isono** I respect you so much. And you are well known as the most powerful lady in the world, so my first…

**Merkel's G.S.** What is the meaning of "lady"?

2　目指すのは「世界平和のための単一組織」

メルケル守護霊　クール。冷静にです。

磯野　わかりました。冷静に。

メルケル守護霊　礼儀正しく。

磯野　はい。礼儀正しく。わかりました。あなたは2005
年に初の女性首相になられました。それ以来13年間、EU
の最強国であるドイツを率いていらっしゃいます。

メルケル守護霊　ありがとう、ありがとう、ありがとうご
ざいます。

磯野　深くご尊敬申し上げます。また、世界で最もパワフ
ルな女性として有名な方ですので、最初の……。

メルケル守護霊　「女性」とは、どういう意味ですか。

23

**Isono** Lady? No, no, I just... [*Laughs.*]

**Jiro Ayaori** Are you saying that you seem like a man... [*Laughs.*]

**Merkel's G.S.** Most powerful "person."

**Isono** Person. I'm sorry. I made a mistake. So, you are the most powerful "leader" in the world.

**Merkel's G.S.** OK. Better.

**Isono** OK. Thank you. So, my first question is, "What is the source of your leadership?"

**Merkel's G.S.** *Denken* ("Think" in German). Ah. Think.

**Isono** To think.

磯野　女性？　いえいえ、ただ……（笑）。

綾織次郎　あなたは男性のようだと……（笑）。



メルケル守護霊　最もパワフルな「人物」です。

磯野　人物です。失礼いたしました。間違えました。世界
で最もパワフルな「リーダー」です。

メルケル守護霊　オーケー。そのほうがいいですね。

磯野　はい。ありがとうございます。最初の質問ですが、
あなたの指導力の源泉は何でしょうか。

メルケル守護霊　デンケン（ドイツ語で「考える」）。ああ。
考えることです。

磯野　「考える」。

**Merkel's G.S.** Continue thinking.

**Isono** That…

**Merkel's G.S.** And make good decisions. That's all.

**Isono** So, when you make decisions, what are the criteria or thinking you have?

**Merkel's G.S.** Firstly, study harder and harder. Next, listen to the opinions of famous people and then listen to the common people. And lastly, please listen to the voice of God and think within you. Obey your conscience and make a decision. OK?

**Isono** Yes, Thank you very much.

**Ayaori** You said to listen to the voice of God. Could you tell us your viewpoint of faith?

メルケル守護霊　考え続けることです。

磯野　それは……。

メルケル守護霊　そして、良き判断をする。以上です。

磯野　判断をする際の基準や考え方はどのようなもので
しょうか。

メルケル守護霊　まずは、もっともっと学ぶこと。次に著
名人の意見を聴き、それから一般人の話を聴くこと。最後
に神の声を聴き、心の中で考えてください。良心に従って
判断することです。よろしいですか。

磯野　はい。ありがとうございます。

綾織　「神の声を聴く」とおっしゃいましたが、あなたの
信仰観を教えていただけますか。

**Merkel's G.S.** Viewpoint of faith? Formally, I'm a Christian. Formally. Traditional Christian.

**Isono** OK.

**Merkel's G.S.** In Germany.

**Isono** But…

**Merkel's G.S.** "But"? But? No, it's a conclusion, so no.

**Isono** No?

**Hanako Cho** What kind of faith do you have right now?

**Merkel's G.S.** I have faith in God. Large print God.

2 目指すのは「世界平和のための単一組織」

メルケル守護霊　信仰観ですか。公式にはキリスト教徒です。公式にはね。伝統的なキリスト教徒です。

磯野　わかりました。

メルケル守護霊　ドイツの。

磯野　しかし……。

メルケル守護霊　「しかし」？　しかし？　それを言うと結論になってしまうので駄目です。

磯野　駄目ですか。

長華子　今はどのような信仰をお持ちなのですか。

メルケル守護霊　神への信仰です。大文字のゴッドです。

29

**Isono** G–O–D?

**Merkel's G.S.** Oh, yeah.

**Isono** So, you believe in the Creator?

**Merkel's G.S.** Yeah, not only Jesus Christ, but God. Printed in large "G".

**Cho** Does it mean El Cantare?

**Merkel's G.S.** You call him so, but it must be the conclusion, so never ask me too much.

**Ayaori** OK. To be frank, your…

**Merkel's G.S.** I can understand your English, so you

2 目指すのは「世界平和のための単一組織」

磯野　G-O-D ですね。

メルケル守護霊　そうです。

磯野　つまり、クリエイター（創造主）を信じているということですか。

メルケル守護霊　そうです。イエス・キリストだけでなく、神を信じています。大文字の「G」で始まる神（God）です。

長　エル・カンターレのことでしょうか。

メルケル守護霊　あなたがたはそう呼んでいますが、それは結論に来るべきことですので、あまり訊きすぎてはいけません。

綾織　わかりました。率直に言いますと、あなたは……

メルケル守護霊　あなたの英語はわかりますので、日本語

can think in Japanese and speak poor English. OK?

**Isono** No, no, no, he's good at speaking English.

**Merkel's G.S.** Really?

**Isono** Yes.

**Merkel's G.S.** Sorry, sorry. I'm sorry.

**Ayaori** It's OK. Thank you very much. Your approval rating…

**Merkel's G.S.** I cannot understand your English.

**Ayaori** [*Laughs.*] Your…

**Merkel's G.S.** Your translation is very difficult. Is it

で考えて、拙い英語で話してもらえば大丈夫ですから。オーケー？

磯野　いえ、いえ、いえ、彼は英語を上手く話せますので。

メルケル守護霊　本当ですか。

磯野　はい。

メルケル守護霊　失礼、失礼。ごめんなさい。

綾織　大丈夫です。ありがとうございます。あなたの支持率は……。

メルケル守護霊　あなたの英語はわかりませんね。

綾織　（笑）あなたの……。

メルケル守護霊　あなたの翻訳は非常に難しいので、ロシ

Russian or…

**Isono** No.

**Ayaori** …approval rating is…

**Merkel's G.S.** Ap, ap… appro?

**Ayaori** Approval.

**Merkel's G.S.** Approval?

**Ayaori** Approval rating.

**Merkel's G.S.** Approval rating?

**Ayaori** Approval rating is falling...

**Merkel's G.S.** Falling.

ア語か、あるいは……。

磯野　いえ。

綾織　支持率は……。

メルケル守護霊　アプ、アプ、……アプロ？

綾織　アプルーバルです。

メルケル守護霊　アプルーバル？

綾織　アプルーバル・レイティング（支持率）です。

メルケル守護霊　アプルーバル・レイティング？

綾織　支持率が落ちていて……。

メルケル守護霊　落ちている。

**Ayaori** … now.

**Merkel's G.S.** Fall in love?

**Ayaori** No, no, no. "Falling." Sorry. Your political power is getting weaker.

**Merkel's G.S.** Ah, I got it. You mean…

**Ayaori** Sorry.

**Merkel's G.S.** … fall down?

**Ayaori** Yes. Yes.

**Merkel's G.S.** My supporting rate…

**Ayaori** Supporting rate.

2　目指すのは「世界平和のための単一組織」

綾織　現在。

メルケル守護霊　恋に落ちる？

綾織　いえ、いえ、いえ。「落ちている」です。すみません。
あなたの政治力が弱まってきています。

メルケル守護霊　ああ、わかりました。要するに……。

綾織　すみません。

メルケル守護霊　下落しているということですね。

綾織　はい、はい。

メルケル守護霊　私の支持率が……。

綾織　支持率です。

**Merkel's G.S.** Ah, I now understand. Your Japanese is very difficult, so… Sorry.

**Ayaori** Your political power is getting weaker now.

**Merkel's G.S.** Getting weaker… Oh, you're insulting me?

**Ayaori** No, no, no, no. This situation is very severe for you. How do you see your political situation?

**Merkel's G.S.** It's OK. I'm old enough. I'm 64. Now is the time I must leave this dirty world. I'll do my best to the end of my chancellor period, but I don't like this kind of dirty and too much emotional world of politics.[*] I studied a logical type of physics or

---

[*]Weeks after this spiritual interview, Chancellor Merkel announced her resignation as the leader of CDU on October 29. She intends to continue her chancellorship until the end of the term in fall 2021, but will retire from politics after that.

2　目指すのは「世界平和のための単一組織」

メルケル守護霊　ああ、やっとわかりました。あなたの日本語は非常に難しいので……すみませんね。

綾織　現在、あなたの政治力は弱まってきています。

メルケル守護霊　弱まって……。ああ、それは侮辱(ぶじょく)ですか。

綾織　いえ、いえ、いえ、いえ。非常に厳しい状況です。ご自身の政治状況を、どうご覧になっていますか。

メルケル守護霊　いいんですよ。もういい年で、64歳なので。もう私としては、この汚(よご)れた世界から去るべき時です。首相の任期が終わるまでは最善を尽くしますが、こんな汚れた、情緒的に過ぎる政治の世界は好きではないので(注)。私は理論的なタイプの物理学などを勉強しましたの

(注) メルケル首相は、本収録数週間後の10月29日、キリスト教民主同盟（CDU）の党首辞任を表明した。首相職は2021年秋の任期まで続ける意向だが、その後は政界を引退する意向も示した。

39

things like that, so I don't like this dirty world.

**Ayaori** What is your goal as a politician or chancellor? What did you want to achieve as chancellor of Germany?

**Merkel's G.S.** My aim is to make the world one organization, for world peace, of course.

**Ayaori** One organization?

**Merkel's G.S.** Yeah, the EU is the first step. And the next step is a world organization more powerful than the United Nations as it is.

**Ayaori** That seems like totalitarianism.

**Merkel's G.S.** Oh, no, no, not so. No, no, no, no. All countries are equal and independent, but they

で、こんな汚い世界は好きではないんです。

綾織　政治家として、あるいは首相としての、あなたの目標は何でしょうか。ドイツの首相として何を成し遂げたかったのでしょうか。

メルケル守護霊　私の目指すところは、世界を「単一の組織」にすることです。もちろん世界平和のためにです。

綾織　「単一の組織」ですか。

メルケル守護霊　そうです。EUは第一段階で、次の段階は世界的組織です。現在の国連よりも力があるものです。

綾織　というと、全体主義のように見えますが。

メルケル守護霊　ああ、いや、いや、違います。いや、いや、いや、いや。すべての国は平等であり独立しています

can argue about their serious problems in a common place, public place, and after their deliberately… they made… deliberately they make… hmm… furious, no, no, no… why is English so difficult... favorly, or… no, no, no… urgently… no, no… arguing… arguing very much, they can make a conclusion. At that time, they should obey the conclusion of the members. That is not totalitarianism, I think.

**Cho** How do you view President Trump's recent speech at the United Nations? Because he stressed the importance of the sovereignty of each country many times.

**Merkel's G.S.** Uh huh, he's a gunman, so he wants to do as he likes. He's threatening the world. It's his way of cowboy. In some meaning, such kind of person is required at the time of crisis, but in the usual period, we must have good conversations. I think so.

が、それぞれが抱えている重要問題を共通の、公開の場で議論し合えるわけです。そして慎重に……慎重な……うーん……激しく、ではなく……なんで英語は、こう難しいのか……好意的に……ではなく、緊急に……いや、いや、議論。大いに議論して結論を出すことができ、そこから先は、全員で出した結論に従うべきである。これは全体主義ではないでしょう。

長　国連における先日のトランプ大統領の演説は、どうご覧になりますか。彼は各国の主権の重要性ということを何度も強調していましたので。

メルケル守護霊　ああ、彼は〝ガンマン〟なので、自分の好きなようにやりたいんですよ。世界を脅してるんです。それが彼のカウボーイ的なやり方なので。ある意味で、危機の時代にはああいう人物も必要ではあるけれども、平時においては十分な対話がなければいけないでしょう。彼は、

43

He is too much self-concentrated person. I think so. If we can have more power, I mean the EU power, we can have an equal conversation with him, but he has a strong power, so it's difficult.

He's dividing the world now and he wants to go back to the age of wars, the war era of the Middle Age. I think so. Now is the day of democracy. He doesn't understand democracy. He just wants to be a champion. So, that's the problem.

**Cho** But Trump's position was to respect each country's independence. And they…

**Merkel's G.S.** No, no. It's a performance. No, no.

**Cho** He really wants each country to bear responsibility for their own prosperity.

あまりに自己中心的すぎると思います。私たち EU にもっと力があれば、彼と対等に話をすることができるんですが、彼の力が強いので難しいんです。

　現在、彼は世界を分断しようとしていて、中世の戦乱期に戻りたいんじゃないかと思いますね。今は民主主義の時代です。彼は民主主義がわかっておらず、自分が〝チャンピオン〟になりたいだけです。そこが問題なんです。


長　しかしトランプの姿勢は、各国の独立を尊重していましたし……。

メルケル守護霊　いや、いや。それはパフォーマンスですよ。いや、いや。

長　彼は、各国が自国の繁栄に責任を持ってほしいと本気で思っています。

**Merkel's G.S.** Yeah, yeah, yeah, it's true. It's true.

**Cho** I think that sounds reasonable. What do you think of his stance?

**Merkel's G.S.** All countries must be or should be equal, but the strengths, I mean the political strength, economic strength and the strength of leaders are quite different. All are not equal as it is.

So, we must have some kind of, how do I say, some kind of help for weaker countries, weaker leaders, and countries of poverty. He doesn't think about that. His "America-First" policy, in some meaning, will be successful for the American people, but in another meaning, it will destroy the world order. I think so.

メルケル守護霊　はい、はい、はい、それはそうですね。その通りです。

長　それは筋が通っていると思います。彼の姿勢をどう思われますか。

メルケル守護霊　すべての国は平等でなければならず、平等であるべきなんですが、強さ、つまり、「政治的強さ」や「経済的強さ」、「リーダーの強さ」にかなりの差があるので、何もかも平等というわけにはいかないのが現状です。
　ですから何らかの、何と言うか、「弱い国」や「弱いリーダー」、「貧しい国」に対する援助が必要です。彼はそのことは考えていません。彼のアメリカ第一主義は、ある意味ではアメリカ国民にとっては成功しても、別の意味では世界秩序を破壊することになると考えられます。

# 3 Views on Trump, Xi Jinping, and Putin

**Isono** Now, you seem to have a severe attitude or severe stance toward President Trump of the United States. So, how can you manage the relationship between the United States and Germany or the EU?

**Merkel's G.S.** The United States, it's in New York, so they are under the control of the United... ah, the United Nations are under the control of the United States of America, so it's not neutral, I think. America's enemy is an enemy of the United Nations.

We need balance. The balance is, one is of course the United States and another one is of course the EU, and the third one might be the Asian power. The Asian power logically leads to the conclusion that it must be made by Japan and China. In the near future, the African power must be added to that.

## 3 トランプ、習近平、プーチンを
どう見ているか

**磯野** どうも、アメリカのトランプ大統領に対して厳しい態度、姿勢でいらっしゃるようですが、アメリカとドイツや EU との関係を、どのようにマネジメントされますか。


**メルケル守護霊** ニューヨークにあるので、アメリカは……ではなかった。国連はアメリカ合衆国のコントロール下にあります。ですから中立ではないと思います。「アメリカの敵」は「国連の敵」なんです。

　必要なのはバランスです。バランスとは、一つは当然アメリカであり、もう一つは当然 EU であり、三番目はアジアの力かもしれませんね。アジアの力は、日本と中国が形成するものでなければならないという結論が、論理的に導き出されます。近い将来は、そこにアフリカの力も加わらねばなりません。

**Isono** How will you make a good relationship between the United States of America and the EU?

**Merkel's G.S.** Firstly, Mr. Donald Trump must learn that American law is not the world law or common law in the meaning of cosmopolitanism and international law. American law is not international law.

It's also the same for China. China's inner law is not international law. Xi Jinping doesn't understand this truth. Both Xi Jinping and Donald Trump, and adding to that, Russian Putin. He also cannot understand. Russian rule is the world rule, he thinks so. These dictatorships must have a chance to learn about the world; world geographic studying and the main rule of international law. They have *Defekt* ("flaw" in German) in that point. They don't have enough common law in them.

I said common law, it's an easy saying, but

磯野　アメリカと EU の間で、どうやって良い関係を築かれますか。

メルケル守護霊　まず、ドナルド・トランプ氏は「アメリカの法律は世界の法律ではない」ということを学ばなければいけません。世界市民主義ないし国際法という意味での「コモン・ロー（普通法）」ですね。アメリカの法律は国際法ではありません。

　その点は中国も同じです。中国の国内法も国際法ではありません。習近平は、この真実がわかっていません。習近平もドナルド・トランプもそうですし、さらにはロシアのプーチンもそうです。彼もわかっていません。ロシアのルールが世界のルールだと思っています。こうした独裁政は、世界の地理学や国際法の中心的ルールを学ぶ機会を持たねばなりません。この点にデフェクト（ドイツ語で「欠陥」の意）があるんです。コモン・ローが十分にないわけです。


　コモン・ローと言うのは簡単な言い方ですが、別の意味

in another meaning, my common law is a law of conscience and of course the law of God. God is not assisting the United States only. God assists all the world, all the countries of the world, so Donald Trump can say instead of the American people the profit of the United States, but it's not enough. It's one part of the common law. Another common law is required to help other countries and other nations of other religions which they belong to. They are lacking. So, even if they have divine nature and charismatic personality, they are tribe-level gods, small "g" gods, I think so.

**Isono** Thank you. Since you referred to the world leaders, could you tell us what you think of President Xi Jinping of China and President Putin of Russia?

**Merkel's G.S.** Xi Jinping is a difficult person, I think

では、私の言うコモン・ローとは「良心の法」であり、もちろん「神の法」でもあるんです。神はアメリカだけを支援しているわけではありません。神は全世界を、世界中の国をすべて支援しています。ですからドナルド・トランプはアメリカ人に代わってアメリカの利益を代弁することはできますが、それだけでは不十分なんです。それはコモン・ローの一部に過ぎません。他の国や、他の宗教に属する諸国民を助けるための、別のコモン・ローが求められているのです。彼らには欠けているんです。彼らに神の如き性質があり、カリスマ性があるとしても、それは民族神のレベルであり、小文字の「g」で始まる神（god）であると考えられます。

磯野　ありがとうございます。世界の指導者について触れられましたので、中国の習近平主席とロシアのプーチン大統領についてどのようにお考えか、お話しいただけますでしょうか。

メルケル守護霊　習近平は難しい人物だと思います。彼を

so. If you want to make him an enemy, it's easy to make him angry and that will make a new war in the near future. But he's very kind to his friends. He has two characters in him, so we need some kind of comprehension between Xi Jinping and us, the world leaders. He's a difficult person.

But if you study deep into the world history, number-one-China era covered almost half of the world, I think, especially in these 2,000 years. So, we must think that the age of China is coming in the near future, more than 50 percent level. We must stand that kind of age. But in another situation, we can control China under the name of the United Nations or under the name of relationship between the EU, Japan, the United States, and Russia, I think so.

And you added Vladimir Putin?

**Isono** Yes.

敵に回したければ、怒らせるのは簡単ですから、近い将来、「新たな戦争」になるでしょう。ただ、友人には非常に親切な人なので、性格に二面性があります。習近平とわれわれ世界の指導者の間に何らかの理解が必要です。難しい人物です。

ただ、世界史を深く学んでみれば、中国が世界一だった時代が世界の半分近くを占めていたと思います。特にここ2千年は、そうですね。ですから、「近い将来、50パーセント以上の確率で、中国の時代が来る」と思っていないといけません。そのような時代に耐えねばなりません。しかし状況が変われば、国連や、EU、日本、アメリカ、ロシアの関係のもとに、中国をコントロールすることができると思います。

それと、ウラジーミル・プーチンもでしたか。

**磯野** はい。

**Merkel's G.S.** Ah, hmm. He's one of the dictators, I think. His dictatorship is very skillful, I think, so I appreciate him in his skill, but his understanding of democracy is maybe 50 percent or so. He must learn a lot from other democratic countries. He is from KGB, so he has a very suspicious mind in him. He cannot rely on other countries. He is apt to think that they are enemies, so it's a problem. It's like China.

But I had several conversations with him and he's a very smart guy. He can think and he can make new rules by himself. So, the country Russia can be made in any direction if he wants. The importance is the intelligence which he gets from other leaders of the world, I think.

The isolation of Russia is not so good, I think. But we are now making economic sanctions with the United States, the EU, and Japan, so he's being isolated, but it's a not-so-good direction.

**メルケル守護霊** ああ、うん。彼は独裁者の一人だと思います。実に巧みな独裁政治だと思われますので、私は彼の能力を評価しています。ただ、彼の民主主義への理解はおそらく 50 パーセント程度でしょう。他の民主主義国からいろいろ学ばなければいけません。KGB の出身なので非常に猜疑心の強い人で、他国を信頼できないんです。「他の国は敵だ」と考えがちなので、そこが問題です。中国と似ています。

　そうは言っても、私は彼と何回か会談しましたが、非常に頭のいい人で、自分の頭で考えて「新しいルール」をつくり出すことができる人なので、ロシアという国は、彼が望めば、どんな方向にもつくっていけます。重要なのは、彼が世界の他の指導者たちから得る情報だと思います。


　ロシアの孤立はあまり好ましいことではないと思います。現在、アメリカと EU と日本で経済制裁を行っているので、彼は孤立しつつありますが、あまり良い方向性ではありません。

# 4 Can We Change the Regime of China, a Country of No God?

**Ayaori** You said the United Nations and the United States, Japan, and the EU can control China. Does that mean we can change the Chinese regime?

**Merkel's G.S.** [*Clicks tongue.*] Ah, it's difficult. They lack the concept of God. That's a problem. Xi Jinping is God. Yeah, of course in our histories, God himself appeared in human history, but in the area of politics, it's very dangerous, I think so.

God who has human nature can be acceptable in our histories, but usually, he or she must be a strong leader in the mindset-changers meaning. The practical political power is not the condition of God and the existence of God's power itself. This political power must be made from the gathered power of people. I think so.

# 4 「神なき中国」の体制を変えられるか

綾織　国連とアメリカ、日本、EU で中国をコントロールできるとおっしゃいましたが、中国の体制を変えられるということでしょうか。

メルケル守護霊　（舌打ち）ああ、それは難しいですね。彼らには神の概念がありませんので。それが問題です。習近平が〝神〟なんです。まあ実際に歴史上、人類の歴史の中に神ご自身が登場したことはありますが、政治の世界では、きわめて危険だと思います。

　神が人間の性質を持った例は、歴史的には受け入れることができますが、その場合は通常、力のある指導者と言っても、「人々の考え方を変える人」という意味でなければならないんです。実際的な政治権力は「神の条件」ではなく、「神の力の存在」そのものではないんです。そうした政治権力は、人々の権力の集合体から成るものでなければならないと、私は考えております。

59

4 Can We Change the Regime of China, a Country of No God?

**Ayaori** What do you think of the oppression to religious groups in China, such as Christians and Muslims? What do you think of the violation of human rights in China?

**Merkel's G.S.** [*Sighs.*] It's difficult. Communist one-party system denies God and religion. They think of religion as LSD or a drug-like thing. In another meaning, they think of religion as a mind-controller, the spring of mind-controllers. So, religious leaders can mind-control their people and it will usually confront with political power and make confusion and conflict. That is the reason he doesn't like religions.

It's from the history of China. In the history of China, sometimes there occurred a political revolution, but in anytime, it occurred from religious leaders. This is their own conditions, so it's difficult to persuade him.

He is, for example, afraid of... how do you

綾織　中国における、キリスト教やイスラム教などの宗教団体への弾圧をどう思われますか。中国における人権侵害についてどうお考えですか。


メルケル守護霊　（ため息）難しいですね。共産党の一党独裁は神も宗教も否定しています。彼らは宗教を LSD か麻薬のようなものだと思っていますので、言葉を換えれば、宗教とはマインド・コントロールをするものだと思っているんです。マインド・コントロールの源泉だと。ですから宗教指導者は人々をマインド・コントロールすることができ、それが通常、政治権力と衝突して混乱や争いが起きる。それが、彼が宗教を好まない理由です。

　それは中国の歴史に由来することで、中国の歴史では政治革命が起きたことがありますが、いつも宗教指導者が起こしてきたんです。そういう彼ら特有の事情がありますので、彼を説得するのは難しいですね。

　彼はたとえば……何と言いましたか……「法輪功」や、

say… "Horinko" group (Falun Gong), or Christian groups of China. They have more than one hundred million population. It's over the communist members in China. It's difficult to deal with, so he is fearing religious groups. You, Happy Science will be next.

**Ayaori** Germany has been building a good economic relationship with China, but in a spiritual message from Jesus Christ...

**Merkel's G.S.** Jesus Christ. OK.

**Ayaori** …and in his message, he said, "Which do you like, money or God?"[*]

---

[*]On September 25, 2018, three days before this spiritual interview, the author conducted a Q&A session titled, "Jesus Christ's Answers In English" at Happy Science General Headquarters. It was a session where Jesus Christ answered questions in the form of a spiritual message. In the session, one of the interviewers asked Jesus about the strengthening economic ties between Germany and atheist China, to which he first replied, "Which do you like, money or God?"

キリスト教団体を恐れています。中国国内にはキリスト教徒が１億人以上いて、中国共産党員より多くて扱いが難しいので、彼は宗教団体を恐れているんです。次は、あなたがた幸福の科学の番ですよ。


綾織　ドイツは経済面で中国と良好な関係を築いてきていますが、イエス・キリストの霊言がありまして……。


メルケル守護霊　イエス・キリストですか。はい。


綾織　その霊言では「お金と神のどちらが好きですか」と言われました（注）。


（注）本収録の３日前の 2018 年９月 25 日、著者は幸福の科学総合本部で「Jesus Christ's Answers In English」と題し、イエス・キリストの霊言による質疑応答を収録した。ドイツが無神論国家である中国との経済的結びつきを強めていることの当否を問う質問に対し、イエスの回答は「Which do you like, money or God?」という言葉で始まった。

**Merkel's G.S.** Of course, money.

**Ayaori** "Of course, money"? [*Laughs.*]

**Merkel's G.S.** Yeah. God said, "Love poverty." So, he's evil.

**Ayaori** But you said you believe in God.

**Merkel's G.S.** Uh huh. Wealthy God is good. It's a meaning of Protestant, you know?

**Isono** It's true. It's true.

**Merkel's G.S.** It's true.

**Cho** How do you see President Trump's policy of imposing tariffs on the Chinese economy? Because it

メルケル守護霊　それはもう、「お金」ですよ。

綾織　お金ですか（笑）。

メルケル守護霊　ええ。神は、「貧しさを愛しなさい」と言われました。悪い方ですね。

綾織　けれども、あなたは神を信じていると言われましたが。

メルケル守護霊　ああ、「豊かな神」ならいいんです。それがプロテスタントの意味でしょう。

磯野　確かにその通りですね。

メルケル守護霊　その通りです。

長　中国経済に対して関税を課すトランプ大統領の政策をどうご覧になりますか。彼は中国の軍事的拡張を阻止する

seems that he wants to make the Chinese economy weaker in order to stop military expansion.

**Merkel's G.S.** Umm, the effect will be half and half. In some meaning, it has influence, of course, but in another meaning, it will make the people of the world poorer and poorer because they must pay more money to buy common things, like food, cars, other electronic tools, or something. So, it's not so good for people.

**Isono** What do you think of President Xi Jinping's plan, "One Belt One Road" initiative?

**Merkel's G.S.** Hmm, it's his ambition. If he were a god, it will be a good policy. If he were a satan, it's not good. Its "road" means his aim to make the countries surrender to him, the countries which are beside or on the belt or road. He wants to conquer

ために、中国経済の力を弱めたいと思っているように見えるのですが。

メルケル守護霊　うーん、効果は五分五分でしょうね。ある意味で、影響があることはあるでしょうが、別の意味では、それによって世界の人々がどんどん貧しくなっていくでしょう。日用品を買うのにお金がかかるようになるので。食料や自動車や、その他の電気製品等ですね。人々にとっては良くありません。

磯野　習近平主席の「一帯一路構想」については、どう思われますか。

メルケル守護霊　うん、あれは彼の野望ですね。彼が神だとしたら、良い政策でしょう。彼がサタンだとしたら、良くありません。その「一路」というのは、他国を服従させるという狙いのことです。その一帯や周辺の国々を征服したいと思っているわけです。彼がサタンなら良くない。彼

67

4 Can We Change the Regime of China, a Country of No God?

these countries. If he were a satan, it's not good. If he were a god, it's a good thing. It depends. [*Laughs.*]

**Isono** Do you think President Xi is a god or a satan?

**Merkel's G.S.** Maybe an ordinary person.

**Isono** Ordinary person?

**Merkel's G.S.** Uh huh.

**Isono** Oh. So, you see President Xi as just an ordinary person.

**Merkel's G.S.** Ordinary person, but has a strength in will. Thinking-and-realizing-his-dream power is strong. It belongs to both god and satan.

**Isono** Germany seems to support the Chinese plan, I

が神なら良い。どちらであるかによります（笑）。

磯野　習近平主席は神か悪魔か、どう思われますか。

メルケル守護霊　普通の人かもしれませんよ。

磯野　普通の人ですか。

メルケル守護霊　うん。

磯野　ほう。では、習主席は普通の人に過ぎないと見ていらっしゃると。

メルケル守護霊　普通の人ではあるけれども意志は強いですね。考えて、自分の夢を実現する力は強いですが、それは神にもサタンにも通じることですから。

磯野　ドイツは中国の計画、つまり習主席の「一帯一路構

mean, President Xi's One Belt One Road initiative. Am I correct?

**Merkel's G.S.** Yeah because he, or China, has been buying a lot of Mercedes-Benz. We got profit from China. So, we are not losing, we got money from China. But China will make inner-side economy to buy and sell the Mercedes-Benz and… I don't know about that. I have no concern about that. *Ich habe nichts zu tun* ("I have nothing to do" in German) about that. But as a country-to-country relationship, we made good profit. So, it's not so bad.

**Ayaori** Last year, Master Ryuho Okawa pointed out that it's possible that the EU and China will collapse at the same time.[*]

---

[*]On February 1, 2017, the author had mentioned the possible collapse of both the EU and China. See Yuta Okawa, *Gendai Doitsu Seiji Gairon* (lit. An Overview of Modern German Politics) (Tokyo: IRH Press, 2017).

想」を支援しているように見えますが、いかがですか。


メルケル守護霊　ええ、彼は、中国はメルセデス・ベンツをたくさん買ってくれているので。私たちは中国から利益を得ていて、損はしていませんので。中国からお金が入ってきています。ただ、中国は国内経済を興そうとしています。メルセデス・ベンツを売買したり、あるいは……よくわかりません。私は関心がありませんので。そんなことはIch habe nichts zu tun（ドイツ語で「私には関係ありません」の意味）。まあ、国同士の関係としては、ドイツは大いに利益を得ているので悪いことではありません。


綾織　昨年、大川隆法総裁は、EUと中国が〝同時に〟崩壊する可能性があると指摘されました（注）。


（注）著者は2017年2月1日、「EUと中国のダブル崩壊」の可能性に言及した。『現代ドイツ政治概論』（大川裕太著・幸福の科学出版刊）参照。

71

4 Can We Change the Regime of China, a Country of No God?

**Merkel's G.S.** Hahahaha, oh, no, no, no!

**Ayaori** What is your outlook?

**Merkel's G.S.** No, no. At the same time!?

**Ayaori** At the same time.

**Merkel's G.S.** Who wants to do that?

**Ayaori** Uh…

**Merkel's G.S.** Trump?

**Ayaori** Yes, Trump is aiming to make the Chinese economy collapse.

**Merkel's G.S.** He will fall in the next election.

メルケル守護霊　ハハハハ、ああ、いや、いや、いや！

綾織　どんな展望をお持ちですか。

メルケル守護霊　いやいや。〝同時に〟って⁉

綾織　同時にです。

メルケル守護霊　誰がそうしたいわけですか。

綾織　えー……。

メルケル守護霊　トランプですか。

綾織　はい、トランプには中国経済を崩壊させる狙いがあります。

メルケル守護霊　次の選挙では落選ですね。

4 Can We Change the Regime of China, a Country of No God?

**Ayaori** What is your outlook about the Chinese economy?

**Merkel's G.S.** Hmm… Now, they are in the situation of a trade war, I mean between the United States and China. Both will lose in the conclusion. So, I'm afraid the world economic recession will occur from this conflict. It can.

**Isono** You studied physics at university.

**Merkel's G.S.** Ah, yeah.

**Isono** And some people criticize that you don't have much knowledge or understanding about economics.

**Merkel's G.S.** Of course, that's right. That's right.

**Isono** Do you agree?

綾織　中国経済に関する展望はいかがですか。

メルケル守護霊　うーん……。今はアメリカと中国の間が貿易戦争状態なので。結論的には、共倒れでしょうね。ですから私は、この争いから世界経済不況が起きることを懸念しています。あり得ますよ。

磯野　あなたは大学で物理学を勉強されました。

メルケル守護霊　はい、そうです。

磯野　なので、あなたは経済学の知識が乏しい、経済学がわからないと批判する人もいます。

メルケル守護霊　それは当然そうですよ。その通りです。

磯野　認めますか。

**Merkel's G.S.** I agree. I don't have much concern about that. But I can read the figure only. It's black or red. OK. I can read the figures of the conclusion of the B/S (balance sheet).

**Isono** So, your basic or fundamental understanding of economics is black or red?

**Merkel's G.S.** Yeah, that's right.

**Isono** Is that all?

**Merkel's G.S.** Yeah. Yeah, my physical legal mind says so.

メルケル守護霊　認めます。あまり関心がないので。でも数字だけは読めますから。黒字か赤字か。はい。バランスシート（貸借対照表）上の決算数字は読めます。

磯野　では、経済学に関するあなたの基本的理解は、黒字か赤字かであると。

メルケル守護霊　ええ、そうです。

磯野　それだけでしょうか。

メルケル守護霊　はい。そうです。私の「物理学的リーガル・マインド」がそう言ってますので。

# 5 Any Good Policies for the German Economy?

**Cho** Master Okawa said that unless Germany is strong in the EU, the EU will not prosper. So, I think the German economy is very important. Do you have any good economic policies?

**Merkel's G.S.** Oh, I'm too kind to weaker people. I have too much intention to rescue the refugees from Africa and Syria, and the Turkish people. So, they say that will make the German economy weaker and weaker. They say so. But I have conscience within me, so it's beyond economy. I must help them. I'm simply thinking that I get a lot of money from China and use it to help refugees. That's all. Very smart and simple.

**Isono** Yes. It's very simple.

## 5　ドイツ経済の良策はあるか


長　大川総裁は、ドイツが EU の中で強くなければ EU は繁栄しないとおっしゃっています。ですから、ドイツ経済は非常に重要だと思います。何か良い経済政策はお持ちですか。


メルケル守護霊　ああ、私は弱者に優しすぎるんですよ。アフリカやシリアからの難民やトルコの人たちを救いたいという意思が強すぎるんです。そのためにドイツ経済がどんどん弱くなっていると言われるんですが、私には良心がありますので、良心は経済を超えているんです。彼らを助けないわけにはいかないんですよ。私は、中国から多額のお金を得て、それを難民救済に使いたいと思っているだけなんです。それだけのことで、実にスマートでシンプルなんです。


磯野　はい、実にシンプルですね。

5 Any Good Policies for the German Economy?

**Cho** But when an economic crisis happened… when the Greek debt crisis happened in 2010, your country didn't really help.

**Merkel's G.S.** Oh, I'm a physicist, so at that time I will leave this position, so I have no problem.

**Ayaori** You strongly insist on instituting an austerity policy on other countries in the EU. That makes negative impact…

**Merkel's G.S.** Negative impact? What do you mean?

**Ayaori** …on the EU economy.

**Merkel's G.S.** What do you mean by negative impact? I can't understand your English. What is negative impact?

郵便はがき

112

料金受取人払郵便

| 赤 坂 局 |
| 承　認 |
| 5565 |

差出有効期間
2020 年 6 月
30 日まで
（切手不要）

東京都港区赤坂2丁目10−14
幸福の科学出版（株）
愛読者アンケート係 行

|ᴵᴵᴵ|ᴵ·ᴵ·ᴵᴵ|ᴵᴵ|ᴵᴵ|ᴵᴵᴵ·ᴵᴵ·ᴵᴵᴵᴵ|ᴵ|ᴵ|ᴵ|ᴵ|ᴵ|ᴵ|ᴵ|ᴵ|ᴵ|ᴵ|ᴵ|ᴵ|ᴵ|ᴵ|ᴵ|ᴵᴵ|

| フリガナ<br>お名前 | 男・女 | 歳 |
|---|---|---|
| ご住所　〒　　　　　　　　　　都道府県 | | |
| お電話（　　　　　　）　−　 | | |
| e-mail<br>アドレス | | |
| ご職業 | ①会社員 ②会社役員 ③経営者 ④公務員 ⑤教員・研究者<br>⑥自営業 ⑦主婦 ⑧学生 ⑨パート・アルバイト ⑩他（　　） | |
| 今後、弊社の新刊案内などをお送りしてもよろしいですか？　（はい・いいえ） | | |

# 愛読者プレゼント☆アンケート

『スピリチュアル・インタビュー メルケル首相の理想と課題』のご購読ありがとうございました。今後の参考とさせていただきますので、下記の質問にお答えください。抽選で幸福の科学出版の書籍・雑誌をプレゼント致します。(発表は発送をもってかえさせていただきます)

## 1 本書をどのようにお知りになりましたか?

① 新聞広告を見て [ 新聞名:                                    ]
② ネット広告を見て [ ウェブサイト名:                            ]
③ 書店で見て        ④ ネット書店で見て        ⑤ 幸福の科学出版のウェブサイト
⑥ 人に勧められて    ⑦ 幸福の科学の小冊子        ⑧ 月刊「ザ・リバティ」
⑨ 月刊「アー・ユー・ハッピー?」    ⑩ ラジオ番組「天使のモーニングコール」
⑪ その他 (                                              )

## 2 本書をお読みになったご感想をお書きください。

## 3 今後読みたいテーマなどがありましたら、お書きください。

ご感想を匿名にて広告等に掲載させていただくことがございます。ご記入いただきました個人情報については、同意なく他の目的で使用することはございません。

**ご協力ありがとうございました!**

5　ドイツ経済の良策はあるか

長　しかし、経済危機が起きると……ギリシャが2010年に累積債務危機を起こしましたが、ドイツはあまり助けになりませんでした。

メルケル守護霊　ああ、私は物理学者なので、その場合は今の地位を去りますから問題ありません。

綾織　あなたはEUの他国に対して緊縮財政を強く主張していますが、それはマイナスの影響を……。

メルケル守護霊　マイナスの影響？　どういう意味ですか。

綾織　……EU経済に与えています。

メルケル守護霊　マイナスの影響とは、どういう意味ですか。あなたの英語はわかりません。マイナスの影響とは何のことですか。

81

**Ayaori** Many other countries don't have enough budget, so they can't manage their economy.

**Merkel's G.S.** But I say that every country like Greece—it's a small and weak economy they have—all of them must stand up by themselves. I said so. They said it's too cold or unfriendly, but I learned this philosophy from Master Ryuho Okawa, so it's correct, I think so.

**Cho** With regard to your immigrant policy, I learned recently that about one-fifth of the people in Germany are immigrants from other countries. So, that's why many right wing parties, such as AfD, Alternative für Deutschland, emerged, becoming powerful. What do you think of this kind of populist movement in Germany?

**Merkel's G.S.** Hmm. In some meaning, it was

5　ドイツ経済の良策はあるか

綾織　他の多くの国々は十分な予算を取っていないので、経済運営ができません。

メルケル守護霊　でもギリシャみたいな国は、どこもみな、小さくて弱い経済しかないので、どこもみな、自立しなければいけない。私はそう言ったんですよ。それは「冷たい」とか「不親切だ」と言われたけれども、その思想は大川隆法総裁から教わったものなので正しいと、私は考えております。

長　あなたの移民政策に関してですが、私は最近、ドイツ人の約５分の１が他国からの移民であると知りました。それが、AfD つまり「ドイツのための選択肢」など、多くの右翼政党が出てきて力を持つようになった理由です。ドイツにおける、こうしたポピュリズムの動きについては、どう思われますか。

メルケル守護霊　うーん。ある意味では想定内ですが、私

83

predictable. But I am the love of the world [*laughs*], so I must help weaker people. Master Okawa will come soon to Deutschland, oh, Germany[*], and he will say the same thing. "To help the people of the world, the poor people, that is the mission of religion. So, Happy Science will supply a lot of money to Germany," he will say so. "I will bring a lot of money from Japan to Germany," he will say so, he must say so.

**Cho** I think one of the reasons your party's supporting rate is declining is because of your policy on immigrants. Do you think you have to reflect upon your immigrant policy in order to gain more power of your party?

**Merkel's G.S.** Uh huh. To tell the truth, I, myself as

---

[*]On October 7, 2018, the author held a lecture titled, "Love for the Future" and its Q&A session in English at The Ritz-Carlton, Berlin, Germany.

は「世界愛」なので（笑）、弱者は助けなければならない
んですよ。大川総裁はもうすぐドイツに来られて（注）同
じことを言われるでしょう。「世界中の人々を、貧しい人々
を助けること。それが宗教の使命です。ゆえに幸福の科学
はドイツに多額の資金を供給します」と。「日本からドイ
ツに多額の資金をもたらします」と。（大川総裁は）そうおっ
しゃるでしょうし、そうおっしゃるべきです。


長　あなたの党の支持率が低下している理由の一つは「移
民政策」ではないかと思います。党の勢力を増すために、
移民政策について反省しなければならないとは思われませ
んか。


メルケル守護霊　うーん。本当を言うと私個人は、質素に


（注）2018 年 10 月 7 日、著者はドイツのベルリンに巡錫し、リッツ・カールトンホ
テルで「Love for the Future」と題する説法ならびに質疑応答を英語で行った。

a human, I like to live poor. It leads to the intellectual life, I think so. Gaining money too much makes people weaker in their brain thinking. So, too much money is a poison, I think so, in reality, in my heart.

**Isono** Are you saying you hate wealth deep in your mind?

**Merkel's G.S.** In reality, I'm not a politician. I think like a physicist, so I don't like secular problems. Donald Trump is a very secular person, you know? He is good at earning money and using money and playing with girls, like that, buy land and sell land and build buildings and sell them. He is good at these kinds of secular matters. But to tell the truth, I don't like those kinds of matters. I just want to think.

生きたい人間なんです。それが知的生活につながると思っていますので。人間、お金儲けをやりすぎると脳の思考力が弱くなるんですよ。なので、お金がありすぎるのは毒なんです。本当は心の中ではそう思ってるんです。

磯野　心の底では「富が嫌い」だということでしょうか。

メルケル守護霊　本当は、私は政治家ではないんです。物理学者的な考え方なので、世俗的な問題は好きじゃないんです。ドナルド・トランプはきわめて世俗的な人間ですよね。金儲けとか、金を使うとか、女性と遊ぶとかが得意で、土地を売り買いして建物を建て、それを売る。そういった世俗的なことが得意ですが、私は実のところ、そういうのは好きではないんです。私は思索がしたいだけなんです。

# 6 Where Did Nazism Come From?

**Isono** OK. You mentioned that you have conscience. So, you want to help poor people.

**Merkel's G.S.** Yeah.

**Isono** Is it related to the German history, I mean Nazism?

**Merkel's G.S.** Oh, I'm quite contrary to Nazism. I hate it. I hate Nietzscheism, I hate Heidegger, and I also hate Hegelian. These kinds of thoughts have made totalitarian system or supported totalitarian system. You usually say, "It's a mistake of Karl Marx," but it's from Hegelian philosophy. Next were Nietzsche and Heidegger.

So, German philosophies made totalitarianism and Hegel's godlike philosophy produced the chosen-

# 6　ナチズムの思想的淵源を分析する

磯野　わかりました。良心をお持ちであると言及されました。なので、貧しい人を助けたいと。

メルケル守護霊　はい。

磯野　それはドイツの歴史とも関係していまか。ナチズムのことですが。

メルケル守護霊　ああ、私はナチズムとは正反対ですよ。あれは大嫌いです。ニーチェ主義もハイデガーも、ヘーゲル主義者も嫌いです。これらの思想が全体主義的体制を生み、それを支えてきたんです。通常はカール・マルクスの間違いだと言われますが、ヘーゲル哲学から来ているんです。その次がニーチェとハイデガーでした。

　ですから、ドイツ哲学が全体主義を生み、ヘーゲルの神の如き哲学がドイツの選民思想を生み出したんです。そこ

89

6  Where Did Nazism Come From?

people thought in Germany and it made anti-Semitism, I mean the anti-Jewish people-ism. Anti-Semitism comes from this kind of Hegelian and Nietzschean thoughts. I think so.

**Cho** Is there any philosopher you admire?

**Merkel's G.S.** Hmm. Buddha is not so bad. He is not a philosopher, but it's not so bad. Jesus Christ has a problem, of course. If he lived in these days, he would be a refugee, Turkish people- or Syrian people- or Egyptian people- or Libyan people-like person, maybe. No goods, no money, and beg for food.

**Isono** I think Germany is prosperous in the economic meaning, but Germany doesn't have a central pole in mentality or philosophy. What kind of philosophy or thinking idea…

から反ユダヤ主義、反ユダヤ人的な思想が出て来たわけです。反ユダヤ主義は、こうしたヘーゲルとニーチェの思想から来ていると思います。


長　尊敬する哲学者はいますか。


メルケル守護霊　うーん。仏陀は悪くないですね。哲学者ではありませんが、悪くないです。イエス・キリストは、やはり問題ありです。イエスが今の時代に生きていたら、トルコやシリアやエジプトやリビアからの難民みたいな人かもしれませんよ。物もお金もなくて食べ物を乞うような。


磯野　ドイツは経済的には繁栄していると思いますが、精神的、哲学的な主柱がないように思います。どのような哲学や思想が……。

**Merkel's G.S.** No, no. We don't need such kind of central pole. From the starting point, Martin Luther of Protestantism said, "Don't belong to churches. Don't belong to the Roman Catholic or one Pope. You, yourself belong to God through reading the German translation of the New Testament. Please read the German-translated New Testament and belong to God by oneself, in each family." That is the starting point of our religion, so everyone is independent in this meaning. We don't need "one-pole system"-like thinking.

**メルケル守護霊** いえ、いえ。そんな主柱などは必要ありません。マルティン・ルターが新教を始めた時に言ったのは、「教会に属してはならない。ローマ・カトリックにも一人の法王にも属してはならない。ドイツ語訳の新約聖書を読むことで、自らが神に属するのである。ドイツ語訳の新約聖書を読み、各家庭で自らが神に属しなさい」ということでした。それが私たちの宗教の原点なので、そういう意味で、誰もが独立しているんです。"主柱制度"のような思想などは要りません。

# 7 "My Dream in the Next Century is 'a Global-Level Government'"

**Ayaori** What kind of vision do you have for the future of the EU or Germany?

**Merkel's G.S.** To tell the truth, I'm not so strong at building new economy. I was born in West Germany, but brought up in East Germany. So I, myself suffered a lot of influence from the old-fashioned Russian style of politics and economy. So, it's very difficult. I'm not a Donald Trump-like person, so I am not so good at selling and buying. Before me, there was Margaret Thatcher in the U.K. She was good at buying and selling because she was a girl of a small store, but I am not.

So, I have a dream and a theory, but it's very pure and so people cannot follow me, I think so. But my dream will come true in the next century. I hope so.

# 7　来世紀の夢は「地球レベルの政府」

綾織　EU やドイツの未来について、どういった構想をお持ちですか。

メルケル守護霊　私は正直、新しい経済を興すのは、あまり強くないんです。生まれは西ドイツですが東ドイツで育ったので、個人的に旧ロシア型の政治経済の影響をかなり受けているので、けっこう難しいんです。ドナルド・トランプのような人間ではないので商売は苦手なんですよ。私より前にはイギリスにマーガレット・サッチャーがいて、彼女は小さな商店の子だったから商売が上手でしたが、私は違うので。


　私には夢も理論もあるけれど、それらは非常に「純粋」なものなので、人々はついて来れないと思います。けれども来世紀には私の夢が実現するでしょう。そう願っています。

7 "My Dream in the Next Century is 'a Global-Level Government'"

**Cho** What is your dream?

**Merkel's G.S.** "Gather a lot of nations and have conversations and make decisions and follow them. And every country, every nation is equal, but they all believe in God and hate war" system is essential. I think so.

**Ayaori** Who will be your God at that time?

**Merkel's G.S.** Oh. The •God of the Earth.

**Ayaori** So, you mean we should have one government in the next century?

**Merkel's G.S.** Hmm, that expression is misleading,

---

•Happy Science has revealed the existence of El Cantare, God of the Earth, who was involved in the creation of humans on Earth and holds the highest authority on Earth. See *The Laws of the Sun* and *The Laws of Faith* (both by Ryuho Okawa [New York: IRH Press, 2018]).

7　来世紀の夢は「地球レベルの政府」

長　あなたの夢とは何ですか。

メルケル守護霊　「数多くの国家が集まって話し合って決議をし、それに従う。あらゆる国や国民は平等ではあるが、彼らは全員、神を信じ、戦争を憎む」というシステムが不可欠であると思います。

綾織　その時に、あなたの神とは誰ですか。

メルケル守護霊　ああ、地球神です。

綾織　では、来世紀には単一政府になるべきだということでしょうか。

メルケル守護霊　うーん、その表現は誤解を招くので

●幸福の科学は、地球の人類創造に関わり地球最高の権限を有する地球神エル・カンターレの存在を明かしている。『太陽の法』『信仰の法』（いずれも大川隆法著・幸福の科学出版刊）参照。

so… We must think about a global-level government. It's not the one-party system of communists. It's quite different. We need conversations. We must reflect a lot of opinions from other countries.

But the problem is, if one country has one vote, the weaker countries have a lot of members, so in the economic meaning, it is unprofitable for stronger countries in economy like Japan or the United States or the U.K. or Germany or France, like those countries.

**Ayaori** Do you mean the United Nations will transform into a world government?

**Merkel's G.S.** Hmm, it would be one possibility. But to tell the truth, the United Nations lacks the budget and the leaders of first level, or topflight leaders because the leader of the United Nations is selected from third countries, I mean not great countries,

……。地球レベルの政府を考える必要があるということですね。共産主義者の一党独裁ではありません。全く違います。「対話」が必要です。他国からの多くの意見を反映させなくてはなりません。

　ただ問題は、一国につき一票の投票権があるとすると、弱小国のほうが数が多いので、経済的な面では日本やアメリカ、イギリス、ドイツ、フランスなどの強国にとって不利益になってしまうという点です。

綾織　「国連が世界政府に移行する」という意味でしょうか。

メルケル守護霊　うん、それも可能性の一つでしょうが、実を言えば国連には予算も第一級のリーダーも不足しているんです。国連のリーダーは三等国、つまり大国ではない国から選ばれているからです。たとえば韓国などです。大統領や首相ではなく外務大臣レベルの人たちが選出されて

for example, South Korea. Not the president or the prime minister, but the foreign minister-level people will be elected. So, their management power is not so high. It's a problem. The American president usually looks down upon the secretary-general of the United Nations. Maybe he or she will come from the weak countries, a foreign minister-level person.

**Cho** What do you think of the concept of sovereignty? Because Brexit happened: many British people wanted to make their country's decisions on their own. That's really the issue here.

**Merkel's G.S.** It's not so good. It's isolationism and a self-concentrated thinking like Donald Trump's. They are keeping their own money. They are afraid of getting rid of their money, from them to weaker countries of the EU or other countries of Africa or Islamic countries.

いるので、彼らのマネジメント能力はあまり高くないんです。この問題がありますね。アメリカの大統領は通常、国連事務総長のことを下に見ています。おそらくその人は、弱小国の出身で外務大臣レベルの人物かもしれません。

長 「主権」の概念についてはどうお考えですか。イギリスのEU離脱が起きたからです。多くのイギリス人が自分の国のことは自分で決めたいと思ったわけです。そこがまさに争点になっています。

メルケル守護霊 あまり良くはないですね。それは「孤立主義」です。ドナルド・トランプのような自己中心的な考え方です。自分たちのお金を守っているわけです。EUの弱い国々やアフリカのほかの国々やイスラム教国に、お金を奪われるのを恐れているんです。

So, the United Kingdom is running away from the EU with their money. But it means too much burden on Germany and France. It's a beginning of the collapse of the EU. I think so.

**Cho** So, you mean the concept of sovereignty or nationalism is not important anymore?

**Merkel's G.S.** Hmm, in some meaning, it's important. Sovereignty or nationality is important. Managing the EU is very difficult. I have been feeling difficulties in many languages and of course the traditions and cultures of every nation. So, from the beginning it was forecast to be very difficult.

But we must resist against this kind of confusion. We must conquer this confusion. We can learn from each other. The German people, to tell the truth, don't like the French people, and of course the U.K. people, the United States people, and the

7　来世紀の夢は「地球レベルの政府」

　ですからイギリスはお金を持って EU から逃げようと
していますが、それはドイツやフランスの負担が重くなり
すぎることを意味しています。EU 崩壊の始まりだと思い
ますね。

長　「主権」や「ナショナリズム」の概念は、もはや重要
ではないということでしょうか。

メルケル守護霊　うん、ある意味では重要ですよ。「主権」
や「国民性」は重要です。EU の運営はきわめて難しいこ
とです。多くの言語があり、当然すべての国の伝統や文化
があるので、私も困難を感じてきました。当初から非常な
困難が予想されていたんです。

　しかし、そうした混乱には抵抗しなければいけません。
この混乱を克服せねばなりません。互いに学び合うことが
できますので。ドイツ人は実を言うと、フランス人が好き
ではないし、イギリス人もアメリカ人もロシア人も、やは
り好きではないし、加えて日本人も好きではないんです。

103

Russian people and, in addition to that, they don't like the Japanese people. These are strong countries in economy, and of course, in the military meaning. So, we cannot sleep well if they were getting stronger and stronger.

**Cho** But due to the globalization, your country also lost jobs. The gap between the haves and have-nots is increasing in Germany as well. So, what do you think of this situation in Germany?

**Merkel's G.S.** Oh, at that time, I want to study physics and reading books and hiking and have fun listening to classical music. I worked a lot. It's enough. So, it's the next person who carries the burden from other countries. It's beyond my power.

7　来世紀の夢は「地球レベルの政府」

こうした国々は経済面で強国であり、当然、軍事的な意味でもそうなので、彼らがさらに強くなってくると私たちは枕を高くして寝られないんです。

長　しかし、グローバリゼーションによってドイツは仕事を失いましたし、「持つ者」と「持たざる者」の格差も広がっています。ドイツのこうした状況についてはどうお考えでしょうか。

メルケル守護霊　ああ、そうなったら私は物理学の勉強や読書やハイキングをして、クラシック音楽でも聴いて楽しみたいと思います。多くの仕事をしたので、もう十分です。他国からの重荷を負うのは次の人です。私の力を超えていますので。

# 8 What Merkel's Guardian Spirit Thinks of National Security

**Isono** I would like to ask you about your view of military power.

**Merkel's G.S.** Military power?

**Isono** Since you hate war, you don't want war…

**Merkel's G.S.** Oh.

**Isono** Of course, we don't want war, but some people said, "We can stop war because we have defensive power." Do you agree with it?

**Merkel's G.S.** In the theoretical thinking, if the United States abandons budget for their arms, it will help the poverty of all over the world. They can.

# 8 メルケル守護霊の安全保障の考え方は

磯野　軍事力についてのご見解を伺いたいと思います。


メルケル守護霊　軍事力ですか。

磯野　あなたは戦争は嫌いで、戦争したくはない……。

メルケル守護霊　ああ。

磯野　もちろん私たちも戦争はしたくありませんが、「自衛力があればこそ戦争を止めることができる」と言う人もいます。この考えには同意されますか。

メルケル守護霊　理論上の考えとしては、アメリカが軍事予算を放棄すれば、それによって世界中の貧困が助かるでしょう。それは可能です。しかし、それと同時に中国やロ

But at the same time, there needs the abandonment of armed forces of China and Russia. At that time, if Russia abandoned that kind of arming budget, the EU can reduce such kind of budget and these budgets can be used for the purpose of helping poor people of the world.

Almost billions of people are lacking food every day, so we can help them. We will teach them, for example the African people, the technology for peacemaking and how they can make their own revenue of the nation and budget. At that time we want to say to them, "Be independent." So, military budget reduction, I mean, make it fewer and fewer is essential for the time being, I think.

**Isono** How can you persuade the world leaders to abandon their military power?

**Merkel's G.S.** The bottleneck is Hitler's thing.

シアの軍事力も放棄される必要があります。その暁には、
ロシアがそういう軍事予算を放棄すれば、EUもその種の
予算を削減することができ、それらの予算を世界中の貧し
い人を助ける目的に使うことができます。


　何十億人にも近い人々が日々の食糧に不足していますの
で、彼らを助けてあげることができます。彼らに、たとえ
ばアフリカの人たちに、平和をもたらすための技術や、自
国の国家収入と予算を生む方法を教えてあげて、その上で、
「自立しなさい」と言いたいと思います。ですから軍事予
算の削減が、当面はそれを徐々に減らしていくことが必要
不可欠だと思います。


磯野　どうすれば世界の指導者たちを説得して軍事力を放
棄させることができるでしょうか。

メルケル守護霊　そのためのネックはヒトラーの件なんで

109

We can't say too much about that. They, meaning the countries surrounding us, usually say, "You are the most dangerous country." They say so. "You produced Adolf Hitler and destroyed the world," so we don't have enough opinion about that. We are in the same situation like Japan in this meaning. But now is the day to reconsider about that. Adolf Hitler was born in Austria, so [*laughs*] it's not Germany.

**Ayaori** But President Trump is proposing that Germany should increase its military budget to two to four percent of the GDP. What do you think of that proposal?

**Merkel's G.S.** Donald Trump is good at thinking money, so I hate him. We don't need any money for defending our country. Love peace and love God. That's cheap.

す。それについて私たちはあまり言えないんです。ドイツの周辺の国はいつも、「ドイツは最も危険な国である」と言うわけです。「貴国はアドルフ・ヒトラーを生み、世界を破壊した」と言われるので、私たちはその点について十分に意見が言えないんです。その意味では日本と同じ状況ですが、今こそ、その点を再考すべき時期です。アドルフ・ヒトラーはオーストリア生まれで（笑）ドイツではないですし。

綾織　しかし、トランプ大統領は、ドイツは軍事予算をGDPの2～4％まで増額するべきだと提案しています。この提案についてはどのようにお考えですか。

メルケル守護霊　ドナルド・トランプは金銭的思考に長けているので、好きになれません。私たちは国を守るために、お金は要りません。平和を愛し、神を愛する。そのほうが安く済むんです。

**Isono** But I think the Western countries fear Russia because Russia was their enemy in the Cold War, so…

**Merkel's G.S.** Yeah, enemy. Yeah, indeed enemy.

**Isono** So, if you want to protect your country and the EU, I think you need NATO. But you don't want to support the NATO system?

**Merkel's G.S.** Ah, the NATO system [*clicks tongue*]. It costs a lot.

**Isono** Yes, it does.

**Merkel's G.S.** Main target is Russia, so [*clicks tongue*] it's difficult. Russia has a lot of nuclear weapons, so NATO must protect themselves from Russia.

We chose China to earn money and to make a balance between Russia and the EU. If we have a

磯野　ただ、西側諸国はロシアを恐れていると思うのです
が。ロシアは冷戦で敵でしたので……。

メルケル守護霊　そう、敵です。まさに敵でした。

磯野　ですから、ドイツとEUを守りたいのであれば、
NATO（北大西洋条約機構）が必要だと思いますが、あな
たはNATO体制を支持するつもりはないのでしょうか。

メルケル守護霊　ああ、NATO体制（舌打ち）。コスト
が高いんでね。

磯野　そうですね。

メルケル守護霊　おもな標的はロシアなので（舌打ち）
難しいんです。ロシアには核兵器が大量にあるので、
NATOはロシアから身を守らないといけません。
　だから私たちは中国を選んだわけです。お金を稼いでロ
シアとEUのバランスを取るために。中国との関係が良

good relationship with China, then the EU and China can protect us from Russia.

**Isono** Perhaps, are you thinking that the EU and China will have an alliance between them?

**Merkel's G.S.** China is far from Europe, so we don't think it's dangerous. But Russia did a lot to the EU, European countries. Sometimes Napoleon attacked Russia, but was ruined. Hitler attacked Russia, but was ruined. They are strong and in every time, they have been enemies of Europe. They have an expansionist idea. They need non-frozen sea, that's the reason, I think so. Give your northern islands to them, including Hokkaido. They will be happy. They can use the ocean.

好なら、EU と中国でロシアから身を守れますので。


**磯野** もしかすると、EU と中国が同盟関係になることを
お考えなのでしょうか。

**メルケル守護霊** 中国はヨーロッパから遠いので危険だ
とは思いませんが、ロシアは EU に、ヨーロッパ諸国に、
いろいろやってきましたし、ナポレオンがロシアを攻撃し
たこともあったけれど、滅びました。ヒトラーもロシアを
攻撃したけれど滅びました。ロシアは強くて、常にヨーロッ
パの敵だったんです。彼らは拡張主義を抱いています。不
凍港が必要なので。それが理由でしょうね。日本の北方諸
島を、北海道ごと与えてやればいいんですよ。喜びますよ。
海が使えるようになって。

# 9 Views on Confucianism and Prime Minister Abe

**Cho** With regard to the military threat of China, although China is located far away from Europe, actually, German companies' technologies are being stolen by Chinese companies.

**Merkel's G.S.** Yeah, that's true. That's true.

**Cho** Don't you think that's a threat?

**Merkel's G.S.** They buy Mercedes-Benz, so we are refunded enough.

**Isono** But they stole your intellectual properties.

**Merkel's G.S.** Yeah, true.

# 9　儒教と安倍首相に対する見方

長　中国の軍事的脅威についてですが、中国はヨーロッパから遠くはあっても、現実にドイツ企業の技術が中国の企業によって盗まれています。

メルケル守護霊　そう、確かにその通りです。

長　それを脅威とは思われないのでしょうか。

メルケル守護霊　メルセデス・ベンツを買ってくれますから。それで十分、元は取れています。

磯野　しかし、彼らはドイツの知的財産を盗んでいます。

メルケル守護霊　はい、そうです。

**Isono** What do you think of that?

**Merkel's G.S.** In some meaning, Donald Trump is correct in that meaning. Xi Jinping or the Chinese people don't understand that they are stealing. They say, "All the countries of the world have been stealing from China. Every invention of China, they stole."

**Ayaori** Papers and…

**Merkel's G.S.** Yeah, yeah, papers and black powder…

**Isono** For making fire?

**Merkel's G.S.** Yeah, yeah. Fire and a lot of philosophies or like that. "China has been stolen," they say like that. "Europe is underdeveloped countries. Japan also." They say like that. "America is a new

磯野　それについては、どう思われますか。

メルケル守護霊　ある意味では、その面ではドナルド・トランプは正しいですね。習近平は、というか中国人は、自分たちが盗んでいるということがわからないんです。彼ら曰く、「世界中のあらゆる国が中国から盗んできた。中国の発明が全部、盗まれた」と。

綾織　紙とか……。

メルケル守護霊　そう、そう。紙とか黒色……。

磯野　火薬ですね。

メルケル守護霊　そう、そう。火薬とか、いろいろな思想とか。「中国は盗まれ続けてきた」というわけです。「ヨーロッパは発展途上国で、日本も同じだ」とか、「アメリカなんていうのは新しい国で、たった２、３百年しかない。

country, only 200 or 300 years. China has a 5,000-year history. They say so. They have China-concentrated thinking, so in some meaning, partly yes in true history. Yeah. China is a great country. They can confront Europe enough in the cultural meaning and of course, a lot of meanings. They look down upon Japan like that. From the viewpoint of China, Japan is like the Crete Island or Greek-like country in the EU.

**Isono** Do you like Japan?

**Merkel's G.S.** Yeah, yeah. Partly yes.

**Isono** Partly yes? [*Laughs.*]

**Cho** What do you think of the Confucius Institute[*] in

[*]An educational institute that was founded by the Chinese government in 2004 in order to promote the Chinese language and culture. The institute has locations around the world, many of them operating on university campuses. There are over 500 locations in about 140 countries (as of December 2016). Some people say the institute is propagating philosophies of the Communist Party of China as well as engaging in espionage.

中国には５千年の歴史がある」と言っています。彼らには中華思想があるので。ある意味、部分的にはイエスです。それが歴史の真実です。そう。中国は大国なんです。ヨーロッパにも、文化面やいろんな面で十分、対抗できます。日本に対しても同じように見下していて、中国から見れば、日本などはEUの中のクレタ島かギリシャ程度の国なんです。

磯野　あなたは日本はお好きですか。

メルケル守護霊　はい、はい。部分的には好きですよ。

磯野　部分的には好きであると？（笑）

長　ドイツの孔子学院（注）についてはどう思われます

（注）中国政府が、2004年より、中国語教育や中国文化への理解の浸透を目的として、大学などと提携して世界各地に設置している教育機関。約140カ国で500カ所以上設立されている（2016年12月時点）。中国共産党思想の宣伝活動やスパイ活動を行っているのではないかとも指摘されている。

your country? I think you have many. Like in Japan and in the U.S. This kind of ideological infiltration in your country, matters…

**Merkel's G.S.** Confucian thought is not a philosophy. It's a teaching, just a teaching. You can learn and learn by heart and understand and just use it. But the German philosophy is thinking, individual thinking. It depends on individual thinking, so it's a little different.

Even Confucianism, you think it's a good one, and you want to ask Xi Jinping to learn Confucianism instead of Sonshi (Sun-Tzu) or that kind of war philosophy, but even Confucianism is a totalitarian attitude. It is a managing system and it builds the nation in one theory. So, it's not so democratic, I think.

**Ayaori** How do you evaluate Prime Minister Abe?

か。たくさんあると思いますが。日本やアメリカのように。ドイツに対する、そうしたイデオロギー的浸透に関して……。

**メルケル守護霊** 孔子の思想は「哲学」ではありません。「教え」です。単なる教えであって、習うものです。暗記して理解して使うだけのものなんです。しかし、ドイツ哲学は「思索」です。個人の思索活動です。個人の思索に依っているので、少し違うんです。

　儒教でさえ、あなたがたは良いものだと思って、習近平には孫子などの戦争哲学の代わりに儒教を学んでほしいと思うでしょうが、儒教にも全体主義的傾向があります。儒教は管理システムであり、単独の理論で国を建てるというものです。ですから、あまり民主的なものではないと思われます。

**綾織** 安倍首相は、どう評価されますか。

**Merkel's G.S.** Prime Minster Abe? Hmm, he's famous because of his long-reigning period. Usually, the Japanese prime minister will change year by year, so no one can understand or remember their names, but Mr. Abe is famous.

It's good for you, but he's not so popular in the EU. He just looks at the United States only. And in my opinion, he is aiming at realizing the re-militarization of Japan. He is possessed by ghosts of Japanese empire army. Maybe.

**メルケル守護霊** 安倍首相ですか。うん、長期政権で有名ですね。日本の首相はたいてい一年ごとに交代して、誰も理解もできなければ名前も覚えられませんが、安倍さんは有名です。

その点は日本人には良いでしょうが、彼は EU ではあまり人気がないんですよ。アメリカしか眼中にないので。私の意見では、彼が目指しているのは日本の再軍国主義化です。帝国陸軍の亡霊に取り憑かれているんじゃないでしょうか。

# 10 Merkel's Past Life— a Great Philosopher Who Sought for Perpetual Peace

**Isono** I'd like to ask you about your spiritual secret.

**Merkel's G.S.** Oh. Spiritual secret. Hum.

**Isono** Before this session began, Master Okawa said "today will be an astonishing day."

**Merkel's G.S.** Uh huh. Yeah.

**Isono** What do you think he means?

**Merkel's G.S.** Hmm. It means I'm not she, I'm not he. I'm human.

**Isono** That means you are an existence beyond the

## 10 前世は「永遠平和」を希求した
　　大哲学者


**磯野**　あなたの霊的秘密についてお尋ねしたいのですが。


**メルケル守護霊**　ああ、霊的秘密ですか。うん。


**磯野**　この霊言を始める前に大川総裁先生は、「今日は驚<sup>きょう</sup>愕<sup>がく</sup>の一日になるだろう」とおっしゃったのですが。


**メルケル守護霊**　はい。そうですね。


**磯野**　どういう意味だと思われますか。


**メルケル守護霊**　うん、つまり私は「彼女」ではなく、「彼」ではなく、「人間」だということです。


**磯野**　性別を超えた存在であるということですか。

sexes or genders?

**Merkel's G.S.** No, no, no.

**Isono** What do you mean?

**Merkel's G.S.** Hahahaha. Yeah, Angela Merkel is a lady now. But her guardian spirit is a man.

**Isono** So, you are a male.

**Merkel's G.S.** Yeah, male.

**Isono** If possible, could you reveal your name, please?

**Merkel's G.S.** Oh, you know. You know my name, of course. All the Japanese know my name.

メルケル守護霊　いえ、いえ、違います。

磯野　どういう意味でしょうか。

メルケル守護霊　ハハハハ。はい。アンゲラ・メルケルは今は女性です。しかし彼女の守護霊は「男」なんです。

磯野　では、あなたは男性ですね。

メルケル守護霊　はい。男性です。

磯野　よろしければ、お名前を明かしていただけないでしょうか。

メルケル守護霊　ああ、ご存じですよ。皆さん当然、私の名前はご存じです。日本人は全員私の名前を知っています。

**Isono** Could you give us a tip or hint? In which era?

**Merkel's G.S.** I'm a philosopher.

**Cho** Kant?

**Merkel's G.S.** Ah, Immanuel Kant.[*] So, I'm not so good at economy. You know?

**Isono** So, Immanuel Kant is reborn as Chancellor Angela Merkel.

**Merkel's G.S.** Yeah, true.

**Isono** Yeah, it's an astonishing fact. It is.

---

[*]Immanuel Kant (1724-1804) was a German philosopher. He advocated critical philosophy through his three works, *Critique of Pure Reason*, *Critique of Practical Reason*, and *Critique of Judgment*. Kant is considered the father of German idealism and gave great influence on the later Western philosophy. The ideas in his book *Perpetual Peace* influenced the establishment of the League of Nations.

磯野　何か手がかりかヒントをいただけますか。いつの時代ですか。

メルケル守護霊　哲学者です。

長　カントですか。

メルケル守護霊　ああ、イマヌエル・カントです（注）。だから経済はあまり強くないんですよ。わかるでしょう。

磯野　では、イマヌエル・カントがアンゲラ・メルケル首相として生まれ変わっているわけですね。

メルケル守護霊　はい、その通りです。

磯野　はい、まさに驚愕の事実ですね。


（注）イマヌエル・カント（1724 ～ 1804）ドイツの哲学者。『純粋理性批判』『実践理性批判』『判断力批判』の三批判書を世に問い、批判哲学を提唱。ドイツ観念論哲学の祖とされ、のちの西洋哲学全体に強い影響を与えた。著書『永遠平和のために』は国際連盟の設立に思想的影響を与えた。

**Merkel's G.S.** Yeah. Your Master predicted so. I have already published my spiritual books…

**Isono** Yes. Spiritual message.

**Merkel's G.S.** … in your group. So, I also am a

『大川隆法霊言全集 第9巻 ソクラテスの霊言／カントの霊言』（宗教法人幸福の科学刊）

Ryuho Okawa, *Ryuho Okawa Collection Vol. 9: Spiritual Messages from Socrates, Spiritual Messages from Kant* (Tokyo: Happy Science, 1999). Available only at Happy Science locations.

『霊性と教育―公開霊言 ルソー・カント・シュタイナー―』（幸福の科学出版刊）

Ryuho Okawa, *Reisei to Kyouiku –Koukai Reigen Rousseau, Kant, Steiner-* (lit. Spirituality and Education -Openly Recorded Spiritual Interviews with Rousseau, Kant, and Steiner-) (Tokyo: IRH Press, 2010)

Kant has been a supporting spirit since the early days of Happy Science. Happy Science has published four books of spiritual messages by Kant.

10　前世は「永遠平和」を希求した大哲学者

メルケル守護霊　そうです。総裁はそう予測されていました。ですから、もう霊言本も出してるんですよ……。

磯野　はい。霊言ですね。

メルケル守護霊　あなたがたのところから。ですから幸福

『カント「啓蒙とは何か」批判』（同左）

Ryuho Okawa, *Kant "Keimo towa nani ka" Hihan* (lit. Critique of "What is Enlightenment?" by Kant) (Tokyo: IRH Press, 2014).

 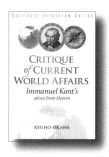

『カントなら現代の難問にどんな答えをだすのか?』（同左）とその英訳版。

Ryuho Okawa, *Critique of Current World Affairs: Immanuel Kant's advice from Heaven* (Tokyo: Happy Science, 2016). The English translation is available only at Happy Science locations.

カントは幸福の科学の初期からの支援霊であり、すでに四冊の霊言が発刊されている。

133

guiding spirit of Happy Science.

**Isono** Ah, I see. Master said you can speak Japanese, too.

**Merkel's G.S.** Yeah, of course.

**Isono** So, that means…

**Merkel's G.S.** *Hanaseruyo* ("I can speak" in Japanese), of course.

**Isono** [*Laughs.*] No, please speak in English this time.

**Merkel's G.S.** I'm *hikari no tenshi ne. Dakara nihongo shabereru ne* ("an angel of light, so I can speak Japanese" in Japanese).

[*Interviewers and audience laugh.*]

の科学の指導霊でもあるんです。

磯野　なるほど、わかりました。総裁先生は、あなたが日本語を話せるともおっしゃっていました。

メルケル守護霊　はい、もちろんです。

磯野　ということは……。

メルケル守護霊　ハナセルヨ、もちろん。

磯野　（笑）いえ、どうか今回は英語でお願いします。

メルケル守護霊　私は、ヒカリノテンシネ。ダカラ、ニホンゴシャベレルネ。

（一同笑）

**Merkel's G.S.** I can speak Japanese because I'm an angel of light.

**Isono** That means you once were a Japanese? You were once born in Japan? Is it…

**Merkel's G.S.** In Japan? Hmm… No, I'm a European, I have been. But Japanese people learned a lot from me.

**Isono** Yes. We studied…

**Merkel's G.S.** Yeah, Meiji period, Taisho period, and Showa period. And now nothing to learn from me.

**Ayaori** Your purpose of being born in this age is to make peace in Europe?

**Merkel's G.S.** I am the origin of the thinking to

メルケル守護霊　光の天使なので日本語が話せるんです。


磯野　では、かつては日本人だったということでしょうか。日本に生まれたことがあったのでしょうか……。


メルケル守護霊　日本に？　うーん……いや、私はヨーロッパ人です。ずっとそうです。でも日本人は私から多くを学んだんですよ。


磯野　はい。学ばせていただきました……。


メルケル守護霊　そう、明治時代、大正時代、昭和時代と。そして今は私から何も学ぶことはありません。


綾織　この時代にお生まれになった目的は、ヨーロッパを平和にするためですか。


メルケル守護霊　私が、国連を創設した思想の源流なんで

build up the United Nations, and the small United Nations is the EU, so I appeared.

**Ayaori** You want a world government in the next century?

**Merkel's G.S.** Yeah, a Kant-like government. We are confronted with the issue of China. You dislike China and have a containing-China policy. But I have an idea of how to steal from China in terms of money. So, we are Dracula to get blood from China.

**Isono** So now, Germany is stealing wealth from China?

**Merkel's G.S.** Yeah, yeah. Today, they want Mercedes-Benz or Germans' very developed technologies or goods, so they admire Germany. But it will make them modernized and westernized. And

す。〝小さな国連〟がEUなので、出てまいりました。


綾織　来世紀には「世界政府」があってほしいわけですね。


メルケル守護霊　そうです。カント的な政府です。私たち
は中国問題に直面しています。あなたがたは中国が嫌いで、
中国を封じ込める政策ですが、私には中国から盗むための
アイデアがあるんですよ、お金に関して。つまり、私たち
は中国から生き血を吸う〝ドラキュラ〟なんです。


磯野　では今、ドイツは中国の富を盗んでいるところなわ
けですね。


メルケル守護霊　そう、そう。彼らは現在、メルセデス・
ベンツやドイツの先進技術や商品が欲しくてドイツを崇め
ているけれど、それによって彼らが近代化し西洋化してい
くんです。ティッピング・ポイント（転換点）を迎えた時、

139

at the tipping point, they will change.

Karl Marx is not a good German, but his influence is still in China. So, they have respect for Germany. Their political thinking is from Karl Marx, so we will change China at the tipping point. So, never mind. I can, we can change China.

Japan already studied Kant's philosophy. It's old-fashion now, but it's really made modern Japanese thinking methods, so at that time, Japan can be a leader of China.

**Ayaori** I think President Trump and Chancellor Merkel can cooperate with each other. That will make the world prosperous and peaceful.

**Merkel's G.S.** He is a man of sex, but I am a man of philosophy.

**Isono** But President Trump was President George

彼らは変わります。

　カール・マルクスは良きドイツ人ではないけれど、今も中国では影響力があるので、中国人はドイツを尊敬しているんです。彼らの政治思想はカール・マルクスから来ているので、私たちが転換点で中国を変えます。ですから心配は要りませんよ。私が、私たちが中国を変えてしまえるので。

　日本はすでにカント哲学を学んでいます。今では〝時代がかって〟いますが、近現代日本人の思考方法を実際につくってきたものなので、時、来たりなば、日本は中国の指導者になることができます。


綾織　トランプ大統領とメルケル首相は協力し合えると思います。そこから世界の繁栄と平和が生まれます。


メルケル守護霊　彼は〝性的人間〟ですが、私は〝哲学的人間〟です。


磯野　でも、トランプ大統領は過去世の一つが初代大統領

Washington, the first president, in one of his past lives.[*]

**Merkel's G.S.** Really? Oh, really? He's a very poor farmer.

**Isono** [*Laughs.*] Yes, but President Trump helps Lord El Cantare's ideas and plans, so please help him and…

**Merkel's G.S.** Ah, he should study more. He cannot understand Kant's philosophy, so he needs more talented brain. He must be reborn again.

**Ayaori** If you want to be in power for a few more years, you should cooperate with him.

---

[*]Spiritual investigations by Happy Science have revealed that President Trump was George Washington in his past life. See Chapters 3 and 4 in Ryuho Okawa, *The Trump Secret: Seeing Through the Past, Present, and Future of the New American President* (New York: IRH Press, 2017).

ジョージ・ワシントンでした（注）。

**メルケル守護霊** 本当に？　ほう、本当ですか。極貧の農民ですね。

**磯野** （笑）はい、しかしトランプ大統領は主エル・カンターレのお考えやご計画のお手伝いをしていますので、ぜひ、彼に力を貸していただき……。

**メルケル守護霊** ああ、彼はもっと勉強すべきです。彼にはカント哲学は理解できないので、もっと才能豊かな頭脳が必要です。もう一回、生まれ変わらないと駄目ですね。

**綾織** もう何年か権力の座にいたいと思われるのであれば、彼と協力すべきです。

（注）幸福の科学の霊査によると、トランプ大統領の過去世は、ジョージ・ワシントンであることが判明している。『守護霊インタビュー　ドナルド・トランプ　アメリカ復活への戦略』『アメリカ合衆国建国の父　ジョージ・ワシントンの霊言』（共に幸福の科学出版刊）参照。

**Merkel's G.S.** I know. Of course, I can be the teacher of Donald Trump, but he will not hear me. He's a bad student, so he never will.

**Isono** OK. The time is almost up, so lastly, could you give a message to the people of Germany and the EU?

**Merkel's G.S.** Oh, OK. [*Sighs.*] Please remember. You, modern Japanese people owe a lot from Germany and now is the time to return it to Germany. Thank you very much. [*Laughs.*]

**Isono** OK, thank you very much.

**Merkel's G.S.** *Mou iika ne?* ("Is that enough?" in Japanese.)

[*Audience laugh.*]

メルケル守護霊　わかってますよ。もちろん私はドナルド・トランプの先生役ができますが、彼は私の言うことは聞かんでしょう。悪い生徒なんで、全然その気はないでしょう。

磯野　はい。そろそろお時間ですので、最後にドイツとEUの方たちに向けてメッセージをいただけますでしょうか。

メルケル守護霊　ああ、わかりました。（ため息）どうか忘れないでください。あなたがた近現代の日本人は、ドイツから多くの恩恵を受けています。今こそ、それをドイツにお返ししてもらう時です。感謝申し上げます（笑）。

磯野　はい、ありがとうございました。

メルケル守護霊　（日本語で）もういいかね？


（会場笑）

**Merkel's G.S.** *Mou, eigo wa tsukareru wa* ("It's tiresome to speak in English" in Japanese.) *Mou iika ne?* OK?

**Isono** *Yoroshii desu ka? Hai. Saigo ni, sousai sensei ga kondo doitsu ni ikaremasu keredomo, nanika, ossharitaikoto toka arimasuka?* ("Is that OK? OK. Lastly, Master is going to Germany, so do you have anything to say to him?" in Japanese.)

**Merkel's G.S.** Please praise Angela Merkel. "She is the greatest lady in the world, this century." If your Master said so, it's enough.

**Isono** OK, thank you very much.

**Merkel's G.S.** Thank you. [*Claps once.*]

**Ayaori** Thank you very much.

**Merkel's G.S.** Bye.

メルケル守護霊 （日本語で）もう英語は疲れるわ。もういいかね？ 大丈夫ですか。

磯野 よろしいですか。 はい。最後に、総裁先生が今度ドイツに行かれますけれども、何か、おっしゃりたいこととかありますか。

メルケル守護霊 ぜひ、アンゲラ・メルケルを褒めてください。「彼女は今世紀の世界で最も偉大な女性です」。総裁がそう言ってくだされば、それで十分です。

磯野 はい、ありがとうございました。

メルケル守護霊 ありがとう。（手を叩く）

綾織 ありがとうございました。

メルケル守護霊 さようなら。

147

# 11 After the Spiritual Interview

(Hereafter, the session was conducted in Japanese. The English text is a translation.)

**Ryuho Okawa** So, that's the truth. I knew it was him, but he didn't tell us until the end.

I'm a bit shocked, too. When I talked to the guardian spirit in the dressing room beforehand, I asked him, "Can you speak Japanese?" "Yes." "Who are you?" He said, "Kant." I was surprised. But I needed to do a spiritual interview with Merkel, not Kant, because we already released a spiritual interview with Kant. I couldn't really let this session be about him.

I don't think she's very good at politics that are deeply involved with actual daily life. She's from East Germany, and communism is theoretical in a way, so someone who thinks like a physicist would be able to wrap their brain around it. She's probably somewhat suited for that. I believe she still has such a way of

# 11　霊言を終えて

（以下、日本語で収録。英文はその英訳。）

大川隆法　ということでした。謎解きが最後で、すみませんでした。

　私もちょっとショックで。そこのメイク室で守護霊に聞いて、「日本語話せる？」「話せる」「誰？」「カント」「ああ⁉」っていう感じになったんですけど、いちおう、メルケルの霊言をしなきゃいけないから。カントだったら、もう、うちでは出ているので。カントの話をしてもいけないしね。

　実生活に密接した政治は、たぶん、そんなに得意ではないでしょうね。東ドイツ出身だけど、共産主義も、ある意味で理論的なところがあるからね。こういう物理学者みたいな頭にでも、彼らはセットすればどちらにでもできるので、向いているところもあるんでしょうね。そういう考え方が、まだ残っているようには思いますね。トランプの、

thinking. I don't think she's too fond of Trump's alchemist-like ability to turn anything into money.

Kant was a lonely philosopher, so it might be hard for him. I'm sure Merkel's life had been a tough trial. The idea at the root of the League of Nations came from Kant. It was based on his book, *Perpetual Peace*. But in reality, the League of Nations failed. Its successor, the UN, is not working well enough. Then, there came the EU, but things are quite difficult. I guess she's being put through both theory and practice.

Her ambitions are good, I guess, but there are many more difficulties in reality. It's hard for things to work out well when you have a couple dozen countries together that speak different languages. Being controlled by something like the government in Brussels is quite discouraging.

A while ago, someone mentioned that it was like having Kobe govern all of Japan. Kobe is better because it might actually be more like Oita. It's difficult

この何と言うか、「何でもいいから金に変える」ような錬金術みたいなのは、あまり好きではないんでしょうね。

　もともとは「孤独な哲人」ですから、今回は、けっこう厳しい試練をやったのではないでしょうか。国際連盟のもとの考え方も、カントの『永遠平和のために』という本から来ていますが、実際に国際連盟は失敗して、次は国連になって、国連もまだ十分に機能しない。EUもつくってみたけど、なかなか難しい。こういう理論と実際とを今、経験させられているというところでしょうかね。

　「志はよし」と。ただ実際は、まだまだ難しいところがあるよと。言葉の通じない二十何カ国が集まっても、そんなにうまくはいかないし、ブリュッセルの政府あたりに支配されるというのは、やっぱり、けっこう厳しいですね。

　この前、誰かが、「神戸が日本を統治しているようなものだ」と言ったけれど、神戸ならいいけど、神戸じゃなくて大分あたりかもしれないというような感じもしないでは

to come up with an idea for all countries. They have problems like that. Ideals need to be pursued as ideals, but in reality, it's not so easy to get the nearly 200 countries in the world all together on the same page.

I don't know whether this spiritual interview will be published or not. She might have already quit by the time she gains confidence [*laughs*], but I would be happy if she were to leave us with some lessons to learn from.

We currently have different opinions on how to handle China. I guess, for Germany, China isn't so dangerous. They can't imagine China launching missiles at them. But Russia might. That's what they think. Our views differ on this, so we must work out what we have to do from now on.

But it's good that such a great empress appeared. There might be a successor to bring prosperity to Germany. [*Claps twice*] OK.

ありませんので。やはり、全部の国のための考え方をするのは難しいですからね。このへんの問題が、あることはあるでしょうね。理想は理想として追い求めなければいけないけれど、現実には二百カ国近い世界の国をまとめていくのは、そう簡単なことではないですね。

この霊言が出るか出ないか知りませんが、彼女が自信を持ったころには、彼女はもう辞めているかもしれないですけど（笑）、何か学ぶべきものを遺してくれれば幸いだと思います。

チャイナの取り扱いについては、少し意見が今、分かれていますので。彼らにとっては、あまり危険ではないんでしょう。チャイナがドイツにミサイルを撃ち込んでくるというのは想像ができないけど、ロシアはあり得るということでしょう。そういうことですから。このへんは少し考え方にずれがあるので、どうすべきか。今後、詰めていかねばいけないかなとは思っています。

でも、偉大な女帝が出たのは良かったのではないでしょうか。そういう意味では、「ドイツの繁栄」ということで、このあとに続く人が出てくるかもしれませんね。（手を二回叩く）はい。

『スピリチュアル・インタビュー
　　　　　メルケル首相の理想と課題』関連書籍

『太陽の法』（大川隆法著　幸福の科学出版刊）
『信仰の法』（同上）
『霊性と教育―公開霊言ルソー・カント・シュタイナー―』
（同上）
『カント「啓蒙とは何か」批判』（同上）
『公開霊言　カントなら現代の難問にどんな答えをだすの
か？』（同上）
『守護霊インタビュー　ドナルド・トランプ
アメリカ復活への戦略』（同上）
『アメリカ合衆国建国の父　ジョージ・ワシントンの霊言』
（同上）
『現代ドイツ政治概論』（大川裕太著　幸福の科学出版刊）

※下記は書店では取り扱っておりません。最寄りの精舎・支部・
　拠点までお問い合わせください。

『大川隆法霊言全集 第９巻 ソクラテスの霊言／
カントの霊言』（大川隆法著　宗教法人幸福の科学刊）

スピリチュアル・インタビュー
メルケル首相の理想と課題

2018 年 11 月 12 日　初版第 1 刷

著　者　　大　川　隆　法

発行所　　幸福の科学出版株式会社

〒107-0052 東京都港区赤坂 2 丁目 10 番 14 号
TEL(03) 5573-7700
https://www.irhpress.co.jp/

印刷・製本　株式会社 研文社

落丁・乱丁本はおとりかえいたします
©Ryuho Okawa 2018. Printed in Japan. 検印省略
ISBN 978-4-8233-0039-4 C0030
カバー写真：EPA＝時事
装丁・写真（上記・パブリックドメインを除く）© 幸福の科学

## 大川隆法 霊言シリーズ・中国の野望への警鐘

# 習近平守護霊
# ウイグル弾圧を語る

ウイグル"強制収容所"の実態、チャイナ・マネーによる世界支配戦略、宇宙進出の野望──。暴走する独裁国家の狙いを読み、人権と信仰を守るための一書。

1,400円

---

# 守護霊インタビュー
# 習近平 世界支配へのシナリオ

### 米朝会談に隠された中国の狙い

米朝首脳会談に隠された中国の狙いとは？ 米中貿易戦争のゆくえとは？ 覇権主義を加速する中国国家主席・習近平氏の驚くべき本心に迫る。

1,400円

---

# 秦の始皇帝の霊言
# 2100 中国・世界帝国への戦略

ヨーロッパ、中東、インド、ロシアも支配下に!? 緊迫する北朝鮮危機のなか、次の覇権国家を目指す中国の野望に、世界はどう立ち向かうべきか。

1,400円

幸福の科学出版

## 大川隆法 霊言シリーズ・世界の指導者の本心

### 守護霊インタビュー
### トランプ大統領の決意
#### 北朝鮮問題の結末とその先のシナリオ

英語霊言日本語訳付き

「自分の国は自分で守る」──。日本がその意志を示し、国防体制を築かなければアメリカは守り切れない。世界が注目する"アメリカ大統領の本心"が明らかに。

1,400円

---

### ロシアの本音
### プーチン大統領守護霊
### vs. 大川裕太

北方領土の返還がなかなか進まない本当の理由、そして「日露平和条約締結」の意義をプーチン氏の守護霊が語る。日本外交の未来を占う上で、重要な証言。

1,400円

---

### 米朝会談後の外交戦略
### チャーチルの霊言

かつてヒトラーから世界を救った名宰相チャーチルによる「米朝会談」客観分析。中国、韓国、ロシアの次の一手を読み、日本がとるべき外交戦略を指南する。

1,400円

※表示価格は本体価格(税別)です。

## 大川隆法霊言シリーズ・哲学者カントの霊言

### 公開霊言
### カントなら現代の難問にどんな答えをだすのか？

米大統領選、STAP騒動、ヨーロッパ難民問題、中国経済の崩壊……。現代のさまざまな問題に「近代哲学の巨人」が核心を突いた答えを出す！

1,400円

---

### カント「啓蒙とは何か」批判
#### 「ドイツ観念論の祖」の功罪を検証する

文献学に陥った哲学には、もはや「救済力」はない──。現代の迷える知識人たちに、カント自身が「新たな啓蒙の時代」の到来を告げる。

1,500円

---

### 霊性と教育
#### 公開霊言 ルソー・カント・シュタイナー

なぜ、現代教育は宗教心を排除したのか。天才を生み出すために何が必要か。思想界の巨人たちが、教育界に贈るメッセージ。

1,200円

幸福の科学出版

## 大川隆法 著作シリーズ・最新刊

# 幸福の科学の後継者像について

**大川隆法　大川咲也加　共著**

教団の始まり、発展と変遷、そして未来へ──。エル・カンターレ信仰を、どのように継承していくのか。後継者に求められる資質とはいったい何か。

1,500円

---

# ただいま0歳、心の対話

**監修　大川隆法**
**編著　大川咲也加　　協力　大川隆一**

妊娠中から生後2カ月までに行われた、大川隆一くんとの「心の対話」。"大人の意識"の隆一くんが贈る、愛と使命感に満ちた心温まるメッセージ。

1,500円

---

# 「UFOリーディング」写真集
## 謎の発光体の正体に迫る

2018年夏、著者の前に現れた60種類を超えるUFO。写真はもちろん、彼らの飛来の目的や姿等の詳細なリーディングが詰まった、衝撃の一書。

1,500円

※表示価格は本体価格(税別)です。

## 大川隆法「法シリーズ」・最新刊

# 信仰の法
### 地球神エル・カンターレとは

**法シリーズ第24作**

さまざまな民族や宗教の違いを超えて、
地球をひとつに──。
文明の重大な岐路に立つ人類へ、
「地球神」からのメッセージ。

**第1章 信じる力**
── 人生と世界の新しい現実を創り出す

**第2章 愛から始まる**
──「人生の問題集」を解き、「人生学のプロ」になる

**第3章 未来への扉**
── 人生三万日を世界のために使って生きる

**第4章 「日本発世界宗教」が地球を救う**
── この星から紛争をなくすための国造りを

**第5章 地球神への信仰とは何か**
── 新しい地球創世記の時代を生きる

**第6章 人類の選択**
── 地球神の下に自由と民主主義を掲げよ

2,000円（税別）　幸福の科学出版

---

# 心に寄り添う。

いじめ、不登校、自殺、そして障害をもつ人とその家族にとって、
ほんとうの「救い」とは何か。信仰をもつ若者たちが挑む心のドキュメンタリー。

### 企画・大川隆法

監修・宇井孝司　松本弘司　音楽・水澤有一　撮影監修・田中一成　録音・内田誠（Team U）
出演・希島凛（ARI Production）　小林裕美　藤本明徳　三浦義晃（HSU生）プロデューサー・橋詰太奉　鈴木愛　大川愛理沙
主題歌「心に寄り添う。」作詞・作曲　大川隆法　歌・篠原紗英（ARI Production）　製作・ARI Production

### 全国の幸福の科学 支部・精舎で公開中！

想像を絶する、
"始まり"へ。

3億3千万年の時空を超えて――いま、
壮大なスケールで描かれる真実の創世記。
この星に込められた、「地球神」の愛とは。

製作総指揮・原案／大川隆法
長編アニメーション映画

# 宇宙の法
## 黎明編

The LAWS of the UNIVERSE-PART I

逢坂良太　瀬戸麻沙美　柿原徹也　金元寿子　羽多野渉　千眼美子
梅原裕一郎　大原さやか　村瀬歩　立花慎之介　安元洋貴　伊藤美紀　浪川大輔
監督／今掛勇　音楽／水澤有一　総作画監督・キャラクターデザイン／今掛勇　キャラクターデザイン／須田正己　VFXクリエイティブディレクター／栗屋友美子
アニメーション制作／HS PICTURES STUDIO　幸福の科学出版作品　配給／日活　配給協力／東京テアトル　©2018 IRH Press

**10.12** [FRI] 日米同時公開　laws-of-universe.hspicturesstudio.jp

# 幸福の科学グループのご案内

**宗教、教育、政治、出版などの活動を通じて、地球的ユートピアの実現を目指しています。**

## 幸福の科学

1986年に立宗。信仰の対象は、地球系霊団の最高大霊、主エル・カンターレ。世界100カ国以上の国々に信者を持ち、全人類救済という尊い使命のもと、信者は、「愛」と「悟り」と「ユートピア建設」の教えの実践、伝道に励んでいます。

（2018年10月現在）

**愛** 　幸福の科学の「愛」とは、与える愛です。これは、仏教の慈悲や布施の精神と同じことです。信者は、仏法真理をお伝えすることを通して、多くの方に幸福な人生を送っていただくための活動に励んでいます。

**悟り** 　「悟り」とは、自らが仏の子であることを知るということです。教学や精神統一によって心を磨き、智慧を得て悩みを解決すると共に、天使・菩薩の境地を目指し、より多くの人を救える力を身につけていきます。

**ユートピア建設** 　私たち人間は、地上に理想世界を建設するという尊い使命を持って生まれてきています。社会の悪を押しとどめ、善を推し進めるために、信者はさまざまな活動に積極的に参加しています。

国内外の世界で貧困や災害、心の病で苦しんでいる人々に対しては、現地メンバーや支援団体と連携して、物心両面にわたり、あらゆる手段で手を差し伸べています。

年間約3万人の自殺者を減らすため、全国各地で街頭キャンペーンを展開しています。

公式サイト **www.withyou-hs.net**

ヘレン・ケラーを理想として活動する、ハンディキャップを持つ方とボランティアの会です。視聴覚障害者、肢体不自由な方々に仏法真理を学んでいただくための、さまざまなサポートをしています。

公式サイト **www.helen-hs.net**

## 入会のご案内

幸福の科学では、大川隆法総裁が説く仏法真理をもとに、「どうすれば幸福になれるのか、また、他の人を幸福にできるのか」を学び、実践しています。

### 仏法真理を学んでみたい方へ

大川隆法総裁の教えを信じ、学ぼうとする方なら、どなたでも入会できます。入会された方には、『入会版「正心法語」』が授与されます。

ネット入会　入会ご希望の方はネットからも入会できます。
**happy-science.jp/joinus**

### 信仰をさらに深めたい方へ

仏弟子としてさらに信仰を深めたい方は、仏・法・僧の三宝への帰依を誓う「三帰誓願式」を受けることができます。三帰誓願者には、『仏説・正心法語』『祈願文①』『祈願文②』『エル・カンターレへの祈り』が授与されます。

---

幸福の科学 サービスセンター
TEL **03-5793-1727**

受付時間/
火～金:10～20時
土・日祝:10～18時

幸福の科学 公式サイト
**happy-science.jp**

幸福の科学グループの教育・人材養成事業

## 教育 ハッピー・サイエンス・ユニバーシティ
### Happy Science University

**ハッピー・サイエンス・ユニバーシティとは**

ハッピー・サイエンス・ユニバーシティ(HSU)は、大川隆法総裁が設立された
「現代の松下村塾」であり、「日本発の本格私学」です。
建学の精神として「幸福の探究と新文明の創造」を掲げ、
チャレンジ精神にあふれ、新時代を切り拓く人材の輩出を目指します。

| 人間幸福学部 | 経営成功学部 | 未来産業学部 |

**HSU長生キャンパス** TEL **0475-32-7770**
〒299-4325　千葉県長生郡長生村一松丙 4427-1

| 未来創造学部 |

**HSU未来創造・東京キャンパス**
TEL **03-3699-7707**
〒136-0076　東京都江東区南砂2-6-5　公式サイト **happy-science.university**

# 学校法人 幸福の科学学園

学校法人 幸福の科学学園は、幸福の科学の教育理念のもとにつくられた
教育機関です。人間にとって最も大切な宗教教育の導入を通じて精神性を
高めながら、ユートピア建設に貢献する人材輩出を目指しています。

**幸福の科学学園**
**中学校・高等学校（那須本校）**
2010年4月開校・栃木県那須郡（男女共学・全寮制）
TEL **0287-75-7777**　公式サイト **happy-science.ac.jp**

**関西中学校・高等学校（関西校）**
2013年4月開校・滋賀県大津市（男女共学・寮及び通学）
TEL **077-573-7774**　公式サイト **kansai.happy-science.ac.jp**

# 幸福の科学グループの教育・人材養成事業

## 仏法真理塾「サクセスNo.1」

全国に本校・拠点・支部校を展開する、幸福の科学による信仰教育の機関です。小学生・中学生・高校生を対象に、信仰教育・徳育にウエイトを置きつつ、将来、社会人として活躍するための学力養成にも力を注いでいます。
TEL 03-5750-0747（東京本校）

**エンゼルプランV**　TEL 03-5750-0757
幼少時からの心の教育を大切にして、信仰をベースにした幼児教育を行っています。

**不登校児支援スクール「ネバー・マインド」**　TEL 03-5750-1741
心の面からのアプローチを重視して、不登校の子供たちを支援しています。

**ユー・アー・エンゼル！（あなたは天使！）運動**
一般社団法人 ユー・アー・エンゼル　TEL 03-6426-7797
障害児の不安や悩みに取り組み、ご両親を励まし、勇気づける、
障害児支援のボランティア運動を展開しています。

### NPO活動支援

学校からのいじめ追放を目指し、さまざまな社会提言をしています。また、各地でのシンポジウムや学校への啓発ポスター掲示等に取り組む一般財団法人「いじめから子供を守ろうネットワーク」を支援しています。

公式サイト mamoro.org　ブログ blog.mamoro.org
相談窓口 TEL.03-5544-8989

## 百歳まで生きる会

「百歳まで生きる会」は、生涯現役人生を掲げ、友達づくり、生きがいづくりをめざしている幸福の科学のシニア信者の集まりです。

## シニア・プラン21

生涯反省で人生を再生・新生し、希望に満ちた生涯現役人生を生きる仏法真理道場です。定期的に開催される研修には、年齢を問わず、多くの方が参加しています。全国151カ所、海外12カ所で開校中。

【東京校】TEL 03-6384-0778　FAX 03-6384-0779
メール senior-plan@kofuku-no-kagaku.or.jp

## 幸福の科学グループ事業

幸福実現党 釈量子サイト
**shaku-ryoko.net**

Twitter
釈量子@shakuryoko
で検索

党の機関紙
「幸福実現NEWS」

政治

# 幸福実現党

内憂外患(ないゆうがいかん)の国難に立ち向かうべく、2009年5月に幸福実現党を立党しました。創立者である大川隆法党総裁の精神的指導のもと、宗教だけでは解決できない問題に取り組み、幸福を具体化するための力になっています。

## 幸福実現党 党員募集中

### あなたも幸福を実現する政治に参画しませんか。

- 幸福実現党の理念と綱領、政策に賛同する18歳以上の方なら、どなたでも参加いただけます。
- 党費：正党員（年額5千円［学生 年額2千円］）、特別党員（年額10万円以上）、家族党員（年額2千円）
- 党員資格は党費を入金された日から1年間です。
- 正党員、特別党員の皆様には機関紙「幸福実現NEWS（党員版）」が送付されます。

＊申込書は、下記、幸福実現党公式サイトでダウンロードできます。
住所：〒107-0052　東京都港区赤坂2-10-8 6階 幸福実現党本部
TEL 03-6441-0754　FAX 03-6441-0764
公式サイト hr-party.jp　若者向け政治サイト truthyouth.jp

## 幸福の科学グループ事業

# 幸福の科学出版

**出版メディア事業**

大川隆法総裁の仏法真理の書を中心に、ビジネス、自己啓発、小説など、さまざまなジャンルの書籍・雑誌を出版しています。他にも、映画事業、文学・学術発展のための振興事業、テレビ・ラジオ番組の提供など、幸福の科学文化を広げる事業を行っています。

アー・ユー・ハッピー？
are-you-happy.com

ザ・リバティ
the-liberty.com

 **ザ・ファクト**
マスコミが報道しない「事実」を世界に伝えるネット・オピニオン番組

Youtubeにて随時好評配信中！

ザ・ファクト　検索

幸福の科学出版
TEL 03-5573-7700
公式サイト irhpress.co.jp

---

**芸能文化事業**

# ニュースター・プロダクション

「新時代の"美しさ"」を創造する芸能プロダクションです。2016年3月に映画「天使に"アイム・ファイン"」を、2017年5月には映画「君のまなざし」を公開しています。

公式サイト newstarpro.co.jp

# ARI Production
（アリプロダクション）

タレント一人ひとりの個性や魅力を引き出し、「新時代を創造するエンターテインメント」をコンセプトに、世の中に精神的価値のある作品を提供していく芸能プロダクションです。

公式サイト aripro.co.jp

## 大川隆法　講演会のご案内

大川隆法総裁の講演会が全国各地で開催されています。講演のなかでは、毎回、「世界教師」としての立場から、幸福な人生を生きるための心の教えをはじめ、世界各地で起きている宗教対立、紛争、国際政治や経済といった時事問題に対する指針など、日本と世界がさらなる繁栄の未来を実現するための道筋が示されています。

2018年7月4日 さいたまスーパーアリーナ「宇宙時代の幕開け」

2017年5月14日 ロームシアター京都「永遠なるものを求めて」

2017年8月2日 東京ドーム「人類の選択」

2018年2月3日 都城市総合文化ホール(宮崎県)「情熱の高め方」

2017年12月7日 幕張メッセ(千葉県)「愛を広げる」

講演会には、どなたでもご参加いただけます。最新の講演会の開催情報はこちらへ。→　大川隆法総裁公式サイト　https://ryuho-okawa.org